Typewriting I

Typewriting Dictionary

Pam Bennett

McGRAW-HILL Book Company (UK) Limited

London · New York · St Louis · San Francisco · Auckland · Bogotá
Guatemala · Hamburg · Lisbon · Madrid · Mexico
Montreal · New Delhi · Panama · Paris · San Juan · São Paulo
Singapore · Sydney · Tokyo · Toronto

Published by
McGRAW-HILL Book Company (UK) Limited
MAIDENHEAD · BERKSHIRE · ENGLAND

British Library Cataloguing in Publication Data

Bennett, Pam
Typewriting dictionary.
1. Typewriting——Dictionaries
I. Title
652.3'003'21 Z49

ISBN 0-07-084992-7

Library of Congress Cataloging-in-Publication Data

Bennett, Pam
Typewriting Dictionary

1. Typewriting——Dictionaries. I. Title.
Z49.B484 1987 651.3'003 87-4113
ISBN 0-07-084992-7

12345 JWA 8987

Typeset by J & K Hybert, Design & Type, Maidenhead.
Printed and bound in Great Britain by J.W. Arrowsmith Limited, Bristol.

Abbreviations An abbreviation is a shortened version of a word. In open punctuation no full stop is required for the following abbreviations:

1 those abbreviations that are acceptable in a shortened form

eg am pm Mr Mrs viz Esq

2 those abbreviations that are acceptable in certain circumstances

Ampersand (&) – never use in text, use only in organisation names and in addresses

eg Preston, Davis & Co Ltd

3 & 5 High Street

Dr (Doctor) – Dr Smith, but 'the doctor said' (doctor in full)

No (Number) – No 421, but 'a number of reasons' (number in full)

Some words are unacceptable in any shortened form and must be typed in full

accom	accommodation
a/c(s)	account(s)
ack	acknowledge
advert(s)	advertisement(s)
amt	amount
appt(s)	appointment(s)
approx	approximately
bel	believe
bn	been
bus	business
cat(s)	catalogue(s)
co/cos	company/companies

Cr	Crescent
cttee(s)	committee(s)
days of the week	Monday, Tuesday, etc
def	definitely
dev	develop
Dr	Drive or Dear
ex	exercise
exp(s)	expense(s)
exp	experience
f	for
ffly	faithfully
fr	from
gov(s)	government(s)
gntee(s)	guarantee(s)
hv	have
immed	immediately
incon	inconvenient/ence
m/c	machine
mfr(s)	manufacturer(s)
misc	miscellaneous
months of the year	January, February, etc
necy	necessary
opp/opps	opportunity/ies
rec(s)	receipt(s)
rec	receive
recd	received
recom	recommend
ref(s)	reference(s)
refd	referred
resp	responsible
sec	secretary
sig(s)	signature(s)
St	Street
suff	sufficient
temp	temporary
th	that
thro'	through
togr	together

sh	shall
shd	should
w	with
wd	would
wh	which
wl	will
yr(s)	year(s)
yr(s)	your(s)

Accents An accent is a mark used to denote stress on a particular letter. If not specially fitted to the typewriter, accents are written in with black pen after typing

eg cliché

consommé

début

fiancé

Accuracy speed tests Accuracy speed tests are set to ascertain how fast you can type accurately. The text is in the form of straightforward copying matter counted in strokes and measured as words per minute (wpm).

Acronym An abbreviation of a group of words to form one symbolic word. There are two kinds of acronym:

1 *letter* eg NATO (or Nato) - North Atlantic Treaty Organisation

VAT - Value Added Tax

2 *syllable* eg Comintern - Communist International

They can be typed in capitals or with initial capital letter only.

Addendum This means something added, the plural of which is Addenda. An addendum could be used at the end of a chapter/book in connection with notes of an explanatory nature. It could also be added to the front of a book highlighting an error or showing matter which had been accidentally omitted.

Address, forms of See **Letters**

Addressee A person or organisation to whom a letter is addressed.

Adjustment of the paper To straighten paper inserted in the typewriter the paper release lever should be pulled forward, thus releasing the pressure on the feed rollers and allowing the paper to be adjusted.

Advice note This may be a copy of the invoice sent to the customer to tell him to anticipate the arrival of the goods he has ordered.

Agenda A list of items to be discussed at a meeting, arranged in the order in which they are to be dealt with.

Ordinary agenda Unless an organisation has its own display, an ordinary agenda is typed to include the name of the organisation, type of meeting, date and time of meeting and a numbered list of items to be discussed.

Items are typed in single spacing, with double between the items. The numbered items usually commence with Apologies for absence and end with Any other business or Date and time of next meeting.

An agenda may be centred or typed in fully blocked style. See **Chairman's agenda** and following example.

Example of an ordinary agenda (blocked style)

THE SOUTHDOWN GOLF CLUB
SOUTHDOWN ROAD
LEEDS   L18 2XY
(Leave 2 clear line spaces)

Chairman: | Secretary:
(Leave 1 clear line space)
S J Prince | L M London
(Leave 1 clear line space)
A meeting of the Committee of the Southdown Golf Club will be held in the Secretary's Office at the above address on Saturday 3 June at 1400 hours.

(leave 2 clear line spaces)

A G E N D A
(Leave 1 clear line space)

1 Apologies for absence

2 Minutes of last meeting

3 Matters arising out of the minutes

4 Correspondence

5 Annual Outing

6 Winter Programme

7 Any other business

8 Date and time of next meeting

(items 1–8: Double line spacing)

Example of an ordinary agenda (centred style)

THE SOUTHDOWN GOLF CLUB
Committee Meeting to be held in the Secretary's Office
at Southdown Road, Leeds on
Saturday 3 June at 1400 hours

(Leave 3 clear line spaces)

A G E N D A

(Leave 2 clear line spaces)

1 Apologies for absence

2 Minutes of last meeting

3 Matters arising out of the minutes

4 Correspondence

5 Annual Outing

6 Winter Programme

7 Any other business

8 Date and time of next meeting

Longest line centred and typed in double line spacing

Alignment The typing of characters in a straight line. If any character appears above or below the normal line of type it is said to be out of alignment.

Alphabetic sentence Sentences which contain all the letters of the alphabet

eg The quick brown fox jumped over the lazy dog.

Alphabetical order The order in which the letters appear in the alphabet

eg A, B, C, D

When several words begin with the same letter they are arranged by the second letter, and so on

eg Benson
Black
Bond
Brown
Bunting

Alternative spelling In the English language certain words can be spelt in either of two ways

eg realise/realize

Inconsistency is unacceptable. In other words, you must use the same spelling of the word throughout each task.

Ampersand (&) This is the abbreviation sign for the word 'and'. Use it only in organisation names and in the address

eg Smith & Jones

2 & 4 High Street

but never in the main text.

Apostrophe The apostrophe is used to –

1 show the omission of a letter in a word

eg don't for do not
he's for he is
six o'clock for six of the clock

2 show the possessive case. If the possessor is singular add 's

eg the boy's name
(the name belonging to the boy)

the child's shoe
(the show belonging to the child)

Proper names ending in s usually just add an apostrophe

eg `James' book`

If the possessor is plural add an apostrophe only

eg `the ladies' feet`
`the girls' team`

If the plural does not end in s the possessive case is formed by adding 's

eg `children's clothes`

3 to indicate feet in measurements

eg `6' (6 ft)`

4 to indicate minutes in time

eg `50' (50 minutes)`

Arabic numbers See **Cardinal numbers**

Asterisk (*) Usually placed in manuscript to mark a word(s) for reference/distinction.

'at' sign (@) Indicates 'at' or 'at the price of'. Use when typing invoices but *never* in correspondence.

Attention line Typed in closed capitals with or without underscore or in lower case with underscore,

eg `FOR THE ATTENTION OF MR J WHITE`

or <u>`For the Attention of Mr J White`</u>

Modern practice is to type the attention line in closed capitals without underscoring, at the right-hand margin, after the date, leaving a minimum of one clear line space before and after it.

Audio typing Normally performed by the audio typist listening to pre-recorded dictation played back on an audio machine. The audio machine is usually operated by a foot pedal which can stop and start the recording as required.

Advantages – Recording can be done at any time, so typist's time is not wasted on a dictating session.

Disadvantages – Transcript can only be as good as the recording.

Dictator must follow strict guidelines with regard to punctuation, paragraphing, etc, and must speak in a clear unmuffled tone.

Automatic carriage return Machines with this feature return the carriage automatically to the beginning of the next line, when the end of one is reached. There is thus no interruption in the flow of typing and speed therefore increases.

See also **Hot zone**

Automatic correction Some machines have a built-in corrector and can delete any typing mistakes when the corrector key is depressed. The correct word(s) must then be typed in that space.

Automatic decimal tab Sets of numerals which include decimal points can be printed in columns with all the decimal points automatically lined up vertically. This is a feature of some electronic typewriters and word processors.

Automatic repeat key Some typewriters have a special repeat key enabling any character to be repeated automatically.

Back spacer When depressed this moves the carriage back. It can be used for

1 Half-space correcting
2 Combination characters
3 Centring of headings
4 Tabular work

Backing sheet A stout sheet of paper which prevents injury to the cylinder through hard typing and gives a better finish to completed work. Essential for all assignments and examinations. If a backing sheet is not available use two sheets of paper.

It is useful to draw a thick black line across the backing sheet to indicate a position approximately 1½″ (38 mm) from the bottom of the paper. When this line is reached the typist can then assess the situation with regard to continuation sheets.

Backward feed A method of feeding paper into the typewriter adopted when a correction/addition is required on a sheet fastened at the top to other sheets.

Procedure

1 Insert a single sheet of paper in the normal way (turning down approximately 2½″ (63 mm)).

2 The *bottom* of the sheet to be corrected is then inserted between the single sheet and the roller.

3 The roller is then turned backwards, the single sheet removed, and the typewritten sheet is then held firmly by the feed mechanism, allowing adjustment and correction.

Balance sheet A summary of the liabilities (what the business owes) and the assets (what the business owns) of an organisation.

Single-sheet balance sheet – rules for typing

1 The left and right margins must be equal and each side must have an equal amount of space.

2 It is probably easier, when using one sheet of paper, to type the shorter side first, omitting the total. This can then be typed at the same time, and at the same level, as the longer side.

3 Leave at least 5 character spaces between the end of the money column on the left-hand side and the commencement of the items on the right-hand side.

4 The totals on both sides must align.

Two-page balance sheet – rules for typing

1 Unlike the single-sheet balance sheet, if two A4 sheets are used the longer side is typed first.

2 The headings should run across the two sheets without a break (when the first sheet has been typed, mark the other sheet with a pencil to ensure that the headings and totals are correctly aligned).

3 When the typing is completed the two sheets are joined together. The typist must pay special attention to ensure that the edges just meet.

Example of a balance sheet

BALANCE SHEET OF XYZ COMPANY

(Leave 1 clear line space)

AS AT 30 SEPTEMBER 198.

(Leave 2 clear line spaces)

	£		£
LIABILITIES		ASSETS	
Creditors	3,361.57	Buildings	7,000.00
Reserve Account	243.00	Fixtures and Fittings	890.57
Capital Account	6,000.00	Plant and Machinery	1,060.00
		Cash in hand	54.00
		Cash in bank	600.00
	£9,604.57		£9,604.57

Double line spacing

Totals aligned

Ballooned words Usually words which have to be inserted into the text

eg I would like to visit you on Monday ⁄ (, 4 December,)
and perhaps we can then discuss the
matter at length.

The above typed out correctly would be

I would like to visit you on Monday,
4 December, and perhaps we can then
discuss the matter at length.

Bank paper Thin paper, lighter than bond, used for carbon copies.

Bible references Should be typed as follows:

II Samuel iv, 2

Bibliography A list of books, articles, etc included in footnotes or at the end of a book, assignment, etc to show the source from which the information has been obtained.

Bill of quantities A document prepared in order to obtain prices or tenders for building.

Ruled sheets are normally used and a new sheet is begun for each separate trade.

Example of a bill of quantities

B I L L   O F   Q U A N T I T I E S

(Leave 1 clear line)

for

(Leave 1 clear line)

ERECTION OF BUNGALOW AT

(Leave 1 clear line)

TOWNEND, CARR LANE, TIPHAM

(Leave 1 clear line)

for MR H M GREEN

(Leave 2 clear line spaces)

ARCHITECT'S NAME
AND ADDRESS

(Leave 2 clear line spaces)

DATE

(Leave 1 clear line space)

NAME OF TRADE CENTRED
eg PRELIMINARIES

(Leave 2 clear line spaces)

ITEM NO.	DESCRIPTION	MEASUREMENTS, ETC			£

Carried to Collection

Nowadays, to save time, many of the above headings are typed in fully blocked style.

Blocked/semi-blocked See **Fully blocked**; **Paragraphs**; **Semi-blocked letter**

Bold print A facility on some typewriters which enables the typist to change to a denser typeface. Usually used to emphasise material within the text. To indicate to the printer that bold print is to be used, a wavy line is placed under the required word(s)/figure(s).

Bond paper Good quality paper used for top copies and letter headings. It is thick enough not to crease or tear easily.

Borders, ornamental Use in programmes, etc for artistic impression

eg

```
-o-o-o-o-o-
   o-o-o
    -o-
```

```
--o-O-o--
```

```
-:-:-:-:-:-

  THE END

-:-:-:-:-:-
```

```
x:x:x:x:x:x:x
:           :
:           :
x:x:x:x:x:x:x
```

Boxed tables In a boxed table both vertical and horizontal lines are employed.

When ruling a boxed table never use a pencil or a pen other than black, although ruling done entirely in ink need not colour-match the typing. A minimum of a half clear line space should be allowed above and below horizontal ruling, and one character space before and after vertical ruling.

Brace A set of brackets aligned under each other

eg

```
(   )
(   )
(   )
(   )
```

Brackets Allow the following spaces after using brackets

eg (1) leave two spaces after the last bracket before typing

eg Next month (February) leaves us without . . . leave one space before the initial bracket and one space after the last bracket

eg girl(s) leave no space before the initial bracket and one space after the last bracket

The full stop is typed inside the bracket if a sentence begins and ends within the brackets

eg (Perhaps Wednesday, Thursday and Friday could be made available.)

Otherwise the full stop is typed outside the bracket

eg The bulletin has been very successful and many students have found the assignments useful (especially Nos 1 and 2).

Capitalisation to be as given This simply means use capital letters only where indicated in the draft.

Capitals

If instructed to use:

Caps – it means all letters are typed in capitals with one space between the words

eg typewriting lessons – CAPS

when corrected is

TYPEWRITING LESSONS

Closed caps – all letters are typed in capitals with one space between the words

eg TYPEWRITING LESSONS

Spaced caps – all letters are typed in capitals with one space between the letters and three spaces between the words

eg T Y P E W R I T I N G   L E S S O N S

Carbons

One-time carbon A thin, inexpensive type of carbon paper, often used for interleaving documents such as invoices, statements, etc. After removal from the documents it is scrapped.

Long-life carbon Carbon paper which can be used on numerous occasions.

Always try to use new carbons for a special assignment or an examination. The 'treeing' effect produced by carbons is caused by creasing. Store carbons flat and preferably in a box when not in use.

If the top left- or right-hand corner of each carbon is cut away it enables the carbon paper to be shaken out while the carbon copies are held between the thumb and first finger.

How to correct a carbon copy Insert a piece of paper between the copy and the carbon paper to cover the error. Erase the error on the top copy, remove the piece of paper and correct the carbon copy. The correction can then be typed.

Correcting a carbon copy with lift-off tape Place a piece of paper between the carbon paper and your copy while you make the correction with lift-off tape (remember to remove the piece of paper after typing the correction). When the document is completed and removed from the machine delete the error on the carbon copy using a rubber (or correcting fluid) and then reinsert the carbon copy to type the correction.

Extra carbon copies When extra carbon copies are required, the name(s) of the recipient(s) are usually typed either –

(i) in the top right or left corner

(ii) at the foot of the paper

The names are usually typed one underneath the other (if there is more than one) and preceded by either the words 'Copy for' or simply 'cc'.

After completion the document is removed from the machine and the individual names are ticked or underscored. Care must be taken to remember that an extra carbon copy is always required for the file.

eg cc `Mr Williams` ✓
`Mrs Dickens`
`Mr Smith`

Blind carbon copies In some instances the writer may not want the addressee to know that copies have been distributed.

In this case when the document is finished and removed from the machine the carbon copies are reinserted into the machine and the typist types bcc at the foot of the document followed by the name(s) of the recipient(s) as above.

eg bcc `Mr Williams`
<u>`Mrs Dickens`</u>
`Mr Smith`

The name of the person for whom the copy is intended is either ticked or underscored.

Cardinal numbers These are 1, 2, 3, etc.

Caret sign ʎ This is the printer's correction sign used to show that word(s) have been omitted. The caret sign appears where the omission occurs.

eg `and perhaps we could meet ⋏ early ⋏ in my office`
`next week`

when corrected is `and perhaps we could meet in`
`my office early next week`

Cases, upper and lower *Upper case* – refers to characters which are obtained with the use of the shift key

eg `UPPER CASE`

Lower case – refers to characters obtained without pressing the shift key

eg `lower case`

Catchword A term used to indicate that there is a continuation sheet. The first word/words appearing on the second page is/are typed at the foot of the first page, preceded by the solidus and ending at the right-hand margin.

eg `at the close of the`
`/festivities`

('festivities' would appear as the first word on the continuation sheet).

When a catchword is a single letter, eg 'I' or 'a' the next word should also be included

eg `in the castle grounds lies`
`/a picturesque`

('a picturesque' would appear as the first words on the continuation sheet).

Centring Text is typed in the middle of the page so that the left- and right-hand margins are equal. Having checked that margins are equal, place the printing point at the centre of the paper, as follows

Elite type	eg	A4 (210 mm × 297 mm)	= 50
		A5 (landscape)	= 50
		A5 (portrait)	= 35
Pica type	eg	A4 (210 mm × 297 mm)	= 41
		A5 (landscape)	= 41
		A5 (portrait)	= 30

and backspace one for every two letters and spaces in the heading. Or add the letters and spaces in the heading and divide by 2 then backspace this amount from the centre point.

Centring over the typing line To centre over the typing line, find the centre point by adding the two margins together and dividing the result by 2. From this point centre as normal, eg backspace one for every two letters and spaces in the heading

eg add margins together
(possible A4 margins – 22 and 82) = 104

divide by 2 104 ÷ 2 = 52

from this centre point backspace the heading.

Chairman's agenda Is similar to an ordinary agenda except that all the typing is arranged on the left-hand side of the paper, leaving the right-hand side blank for the insertion of notes. A smaller left-hand margin is used and the item numbers are repeated on the right-hand side of the paper. (See example on page 20.)

Character pitch selector This allows you to choose which pitch you require. Most electronic typewriters give a choice of three different pitches. The setting equals the number of characters per inch, eg 10, 12 or 15.

Example of a chairman's agenda

THE SOUTHDOWN GOLF CLUB
SOUTHDOWN ROAD
LEEDS L18 2XY

(Leave 2 clear line spaces)

A Committee Meeting of THE SOUTHDOWN GOLF CLUB will be held in the Secretary's Office on Saturday 3 June at 1400 hours.

(Leave 1 clear line space)

AGENDA		NOTES	
(Leave 1 clear line space)			
1	Ask the Secretary, Mr London, to read apologies	1	
(1 clear line space)			
2	Ask Mr London to read minutes of last meeting	2	
3	Matters arising out of minutes. Anticipated questions on	3	
	i Annual Competition		i
	ii Fixtures		ii
4	Correspondence	4	
5	Annual Outing	5	
	i Coach hire		i
	ii Catering Arrangements		ii
6	Winter Programme	6	
7	Any other business	7	
8	Date and time of next meeting	8	
9	Chairman to declare meeting closed	9	

Chronological order Items arranged in the order of occurrence, ie beginning with the earliest date and progressing to the most recent.

Circular letters Identical letters sent to a number of people.

The date on a circular letter can be typed in a number of ways

(i) in open punctuation – 3 May 1986
in full punctuation – 3rd May, 1986

depending on the style adopted in the circular letter

(ii) month and year only

(iii) Date as postmark – typed in the position where you would type the date.

Sometimes space is left for the name and address of the addressee but quite often this is not inserted. If the name and address is not to be inserted then leave a minimum of one clear line space after the date and commence the salutation.

For indication of a tear-off slip you can use

spaced/unspaced dots,
the underscore key
or
the hyphen key

All the lines must be typed from edge to edge of the paper with at least one clear line space above and below. On an electronic typewriter the repeat key is very useful for this.

Where details will have to be inserted use double spacing for the dotted lines.

When typing forms with dotted lines, leave at least one character space after typing before commencing the dotted line, and at least one character space after the dotted line if further typing is required.

Example of a circular letter

Date as postmark

(Leave 6 clear line spaces)

Dear Member
(Leave 1 clear line space)

First of all, apologies to anyone who has been waiting expectantly for the arrival on his or her desk of the second edition of the Register of Assignments, which was, of course, planned for September. I have to report that printing is now complete and you can anticipate the arrival of your copy in October.

I am pleased to report another successful event in Wakefield on 5 September, when Jim Page of Leeds Polytechnic, and a regular contributor to the Magazine, gave a most helpful and instructive talk on Electronic Time Study.

The next event in the Southern Sub-Group calendar is slightly different in that it is a full-day event designed specifically to provide a training opportunity for the Society's membership. Because of the nature of the course, it is necessary to place a limit of 12 on the numbers attending. Allocation will be on a "first come, first served" basis, so please contact me as soon as possible to reserve your place.

I am sure we can look forward to a most useful and rewarding event. Please make every effort either to attend yourself, or to send a representative who you think will benefit from the course.

Yours faithfully

(Leave 4 clear line spaces)

J MASON
Secretary

Circumflex accent An accent in the shape of an inverted 'v' positioned over a French character, usually a or o.

Clear line spacing Always turn up one more line than instructed when clear line spacing is indicated.

For example, if instructed to leave 1 clear line space, turn up 2, that is one clear line and one to type on.

eg 2 clear lines = turn up 3 single line spaces
3 clear lines = turn up 4 single line spaces

c/o This means 'Care of' and is always typed in the abbreviated form. All the following combinations are acceptable

C/o c/o $^{c}/_{o}$ $^{C}/_{o}$

Combination characters (special signs/symbols) Some characters are not provided on the keyboard but can be produced by combining two characters, ie by typing one character, backspacing and then typing the second character in the same space

eg ! Apostrophe and full stop for the exclamation mark

In some cases the interliner must be used to allow the characters to be raised or lowered. See **Interliner**

Commercial signs/symbols Commercial signs provided on a standard keyboard are

pound sign	£
per cent sign	%
ampersand	&
solidus/oblique sign	/
at	@
and the usual fractions	

Complimentary close The complimentary close is the name given to Yours faithfully/sincerely. It is sometimes followed by the name of the firm typed in capitals.

Complimentary slip Often a firm will have its own supply of complimentary slips printed but where this is not the case, a piece of A6 bond paper (half A5) is used with the words 'With the compliments of... (name of person or firm)' typed in the centre.

Compound numbers Numbers from twenty-one to ninety-nine are known as compound numbers. When typed as words they are hyphenated.

Continuation sheets *Continuous text* A continuation sheet in continuous text is typed as follows

Fully blocked layout (Figure 1)

1 Leave 3 clear line spaces from the top of the paper

2 Type the page number at the left-hand margin

3 Leave 2 clear line spaces before continuing

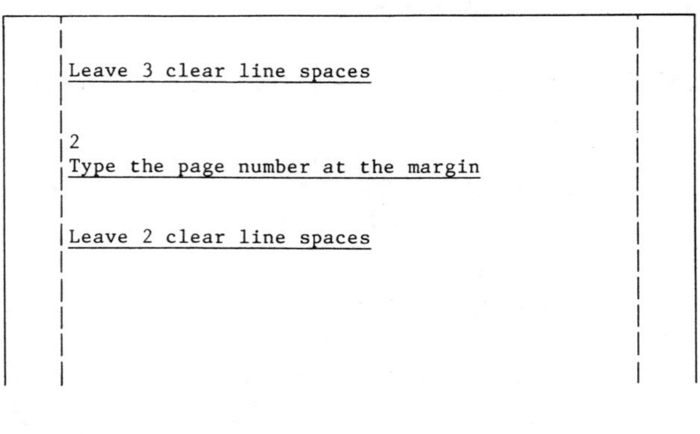

Figure 1 Fully blocked layout

Semi-blocked layout (Figure 2)

1 Leave 3 clear line spaces from the top of the paper

2 Centre the page number over the typing line
(See **Centring over the typing line**)

3 Leave 2 clear line spaces before continuing

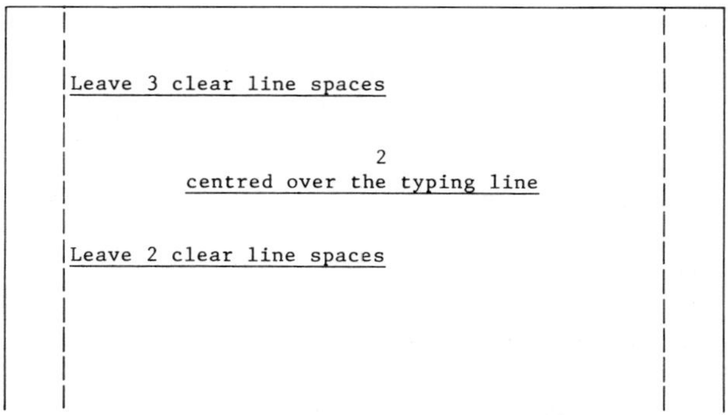

Figure 2 Semi-blocked layout

A continuation sheet in a letter is typed as follows

Fully blocked layout (Figure 3)

1 Leave 3 clear line spaces from the top of the paper

2 Type the page number at the left-hand margin

3 Leave 1 clear line space

4 Type the date at the left-hand margin

5 Leave 1 clear line space

6 Type the name of the addressee at the left-hand margin

7 Leave 2 clear line spaces before continuing

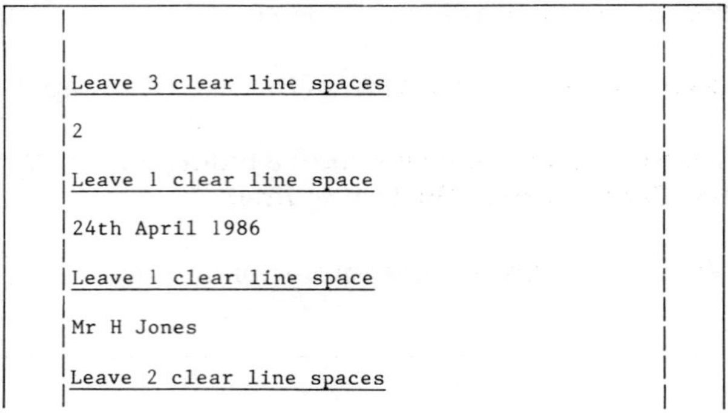

Figure 3 Fully blocked layout with open punctuation

Semi-blocked layout (Figure 4)

1 Leave 3 clear line spaces from the top of the paper

2 Type the name of the addressee at the left-hand margin

3 On the same line of type centre the page number over the typing line (See **Centring over the typing line)**

4 The date is then justified from the right-hand margin (See **Justified right-hand margin)**

5 Leave 2 clear line spaces before continuing

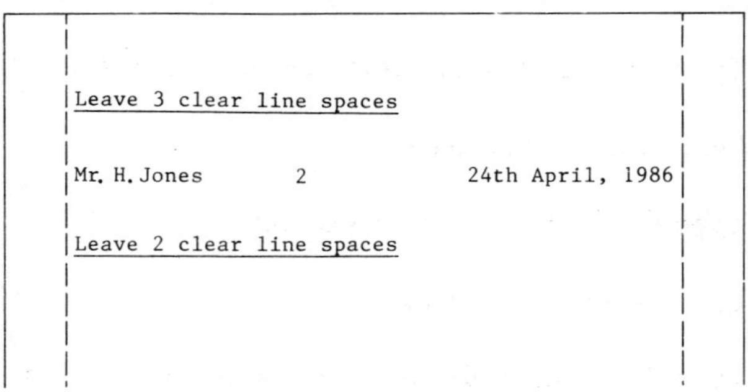

Figure 4 Semi-blocked layout with full punctuation

Ensure that typing on a continuation sheet extends to at least a second line.

The continuation sheet should always be plain paper but matching in size and/or colour the headed sheet.

When typing on the back of headed paper ensure that it is not inserted upside down in the machine.

Copy To distinguish a copy of a document from an original, type the word 'COPY' in capitals at the top and the word 'SIGNED' before the signature if applicable.

Copyholder A device to hold the paper from which you are copying work. Can be free standing on the desk or attached to the typewriter, with a line finder which moves down the page when you press a foot pedal. The advantage of a copyholder is that it brings the matter to the level of the eyes and saves straining.

Copying, from a book, paper, etc The best position for copying is to place the book, etc square in front of the eyes. Where this is not possible it is best placed to the right of the typewriter.

Corrections *Using a rubber* Take the carriage to whichever side of the machine is convenient and gently remove the error, blowing away rubber dust as you rub up and down.

Using correction paper Place the strip of correction paper in front of the printing point over the error and type once again the incorrect letter. The incorrect letter will now be covered by a film of powder and you can type the correct letter on the top.

Using correction fluid Paint the error with the fluid and allow to dry thoroughly before typing the correction. Make sure that the correction fluid is not too thick or lumpy and that the whole error is covered.

Some examination boards penalise the use of white correction fluid on coloured paper – use a rubber. However, a variety of coloured fluids are now available which match the usual coloured papers, and these are quite permissable. Always ensure the correction is clean and neat.

Correcting ribbons

Lift-off ribbons These 'lift-off' the mistake from the typed page to leave the paper clear for the correction. Used with a carbon ribbon.

Cover-up ribbon These cover up the error and are for use with a fabric ribbon.

See also **Half-space correcting**

Correction signs

trs — transpose, change the order

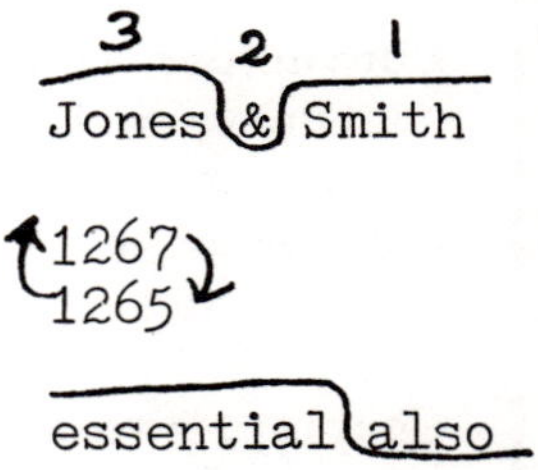

NP or ‖ or [— new paragraph

close up, no space required

Run on — do not start a new paragraph

stet — let it stand; when two words are crossed out it is always the rule to type the one with the dots underneath

eg ~~normal~~ ~~average~~ ✓

lc — lower case - small letters

uc — upper case - capital letters

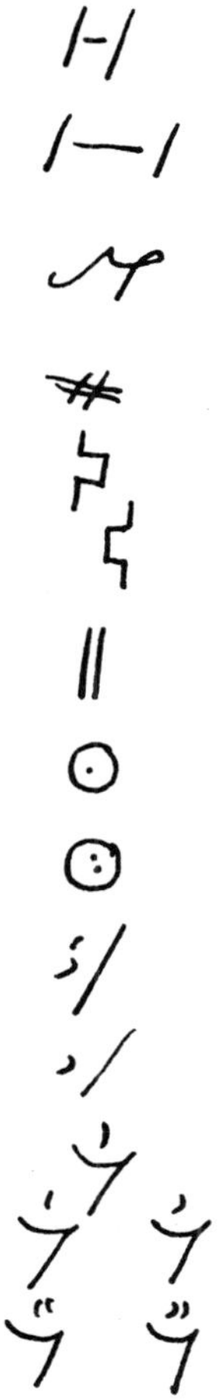

insert a hyphen

insert a dash

delete - do not type the words crossed out

space required

move text to the left

move text to the right

straighten margin

insert full stop

insert colon

insert semi-colon

insert comma

insert apostrophe

insert single quotation marks

insert double quotation marks

CAPS use capital letters

Courtesy titles A courtesy title must always be used with a person's name.

For a man you can use *one* of the following

Mr
Esq
or Rev if applicable

For a woman you can use whichever of the following is applicable

Miss
Ms
Mrs

Messrs is used before the name of a partnership

eg Messrs Brown & Sons

A courtesy title should not be used in the following cases

1 Before the name of a limited company

eg J Black & Co Ltd

2 With impersonal names

eg The Metal Box Co

3 When a title is used in a name

eg Sir Thomas Black & Co

Cover The typewriter should always be covered when not in use.

Cursor A flashing square, oblong or line which indicates your position on a visual display screen.

Dagger A dagger or double dagger is used to draw the reader's attention to a footnote

eg ‡
or
eg ‡

Daisywheel A printing element made of plastic or metal which looks like a flattened daisy. The characters are placed around the circumference of the wheel, each one occupying a spoke or petal, as they are sometimes called.

Dash Always leave a space before and after typing a dash

eg game - in fact

each morning - except Wednesday

Date Typists are generally expected to type the appropriate date on all letters and memos, unless told otherwise.

Dead keys Some machines are provided with keys which, when depressed, do not cause the carriage to move forward the usual single character space. These are known as 'dead keys' and may be specially fitted to a typewriter, usually replacing keys for fractions.

Debit note This document indicates to the customer that he was undercharged on certain item(s) and owes the supplier more than was stated on the invoice.

Decimal point The decimal point is usually typed in the normal position of the full stop, with no space before or after

eg 20.5

Where a number is less than one, a nought must precede the decimal point

eg 0.75

Degree sign To create the degree sign type a small 'o' raised half a space above the typing line

eg 90°

There is no space between the figure and the degree sign when it is typed on its own but when followed by C (Centigrade/Celsius) or F (Fahrenheit) there is a space between the figures and the degree sign but no space between the degree sign and letter C or F.

eg $90\ ^{o}F$

Delete as applicable This means cross/take out material marked as unwanted.

Delete sign The delete sign  is sometimes written in the margin when letters or words have to be omitted.

Delivery note A delivery note is similar to an advice note and is often a copy of the invoice, although no prices are indicated. A delivery note is usually packed with the goods so that the recipient can check that all items listed have been received.

Diagonal headings To type diagonal headings the paper is inserted diagonally and the heading must be typed parallel to the diagonal lines and centred between the two. It is easier to type the headings and rule the diagonal lines after typing the tabulation, remembering that the diagonal lines should be aligned with the alignment scale when the paper is reinserted.

To type diagonal headings:

1 Calculate the horizontal spaces required for the column items and spaces between the columns, (if possible making all the diagonal heading columns the same width). Rule, by using the underscore, the top horizontal line or mark the beginning and the end.

2 Calculate the number of vertical line spaces required for the headings (See **Vertical headings).** Turn up the correct amount and rule the second horizontal line.

3 Using the second horizontal line, mark in pencil the scale points for the vertical lines between the columns (this will correspond with the scale points for the bottom of the diagonal lines). Set tabulator stops for the start of each column as usual.

4 Proceed to make the scale points for the top of the diagonal lines. The top of the first diagonal line should be marked at the same scale point as the second vertical line, the second as the third, and so on. To mark the top of the last diagonal

line, tap the space bar once for the number of spaces required for the longest line of the column, plus three extra spaces (for the spaces between the columns) and mark accordingly. (See also **Tabulation**.)

Disengaging the ribbon *Manual machines* Move the ribbon position indicator to the white marker. When the ribbon is disengaged the typebars come into direct contact with the paper. The ribbon should always be disengaged when typing stencils on manual typewriters. Also it is advisable to disengage the ribbon to check position and alignment before typing in any correction after erasing.

Electronic machines Switch the machine off and remove the ribbon.

Ditto marks These can be double quotation marks (") under each word or

```
do   do.   -do-   - do -   ditto
```

under a group of words.

Remember to be consistent. Ditto marks are typed under the first letter of the word in fully blocked layout or centred under each word for semi-blocked layout.

Fully blocked

```
January
"
```

Semi-blocked

```
black or brown
  "    "    "
```

Division of words at line endings

Divide – *according to syllables*

eg `pen-cil` `type-writer`

between double consonants

eg `din-ner` `sup-pose`

after a prefix or before a suffix

eg `con-fine` `improve-ment`

already hyphenated and compound words at the hyphen

eg `part-time` `pre-eminent`

so as not to change the pronunciation

eg `chil-dren not child-ren`

Do not divide – *within a single syllable word and its plural*

eg `case cases` `piece pieces`

Proper names

eg `London` `Jones`

at a point which would allow only two letters to be taken to the next line

eg `signed not sign-ed`

within figures

on more than two consecutive lines

numbers or courtesy titles from the words to which they refer

the last word of a page or paragraph.

WHEN IN DOUBT – DO NOT DIVIDE

Double quotation marks Used to mark the actual words spoken. No space is left between quotation marks and the speech they are enclosing

eg `"This is mine", said James.`

Draft A first rough copy of any handwritten document. Typed in double or treble spacing with wide side margins to allow for extensive revision. Usually the word 'DRAFT' appears at the top left-hand side of the paper.

Dropped head This term is given to the practice of using a deeper top margin on the first page of typed matter. It is used for titles and chapters. The first page commences approximately 2½″ (63 mm) down instead of the usual 1″ (25 mm).

E & O E See **Invoices**

Elision The omission of a letter (usually a vowel) when pronouncing a word

eg `couldn't`

Only use when quoting direct speech.

Elite type A type size on some typewriters that produces 12 characters to 1″ (25 mm).

Ellipsis Words are sometimes deliberately omitted at the beginning, in the middle, or at the end of a sentence.

This omission, called an ellipsis, is indicated by the use of 3 spaced/unspaced full stops, bearing in mind the following rules

Ellipsis at the beginning of a sentence – the full stop is typed at the end of the previous sentence as usual and followed by one space after the full stop and three spaced/unspaced dots

Ellipsis in the middle of a sentence	– one space plus three spaced/unspaced dots
Ellipsis at the end of a sentence	– the three spaced/unspaced dots are followed by a fourth dot to show the end of a sentence.

REMEMBER TO BE CONSISTENT.

Enclosure The inclusion of papers or documents in a letter or memo is indicated by typing the abbreviation 'Enc' at the left-hand margin at least one clear line space below the designation. When more than one item is enclosed 'Encs' is typed.

Marginal note for enclosure Some typists prefer to make a note in the margin to serve as a reminder.

Marginal notes can be		
	dots	...
	dashes	---
	strokes	///

A minimum of three must be used and at least one space left after the marks before the line of type.

It is worth noting, however, that some examining bodies say that 'Enc' should not be used if the word 'attached' is used in the body of the letter.

End of paper Always leave approximately 1″ (25 mm) of space at the foot of the paper. The most widely-used method to ensure this is to make a pencil mark slightly above the correct distance from the foot of the paper. When this mark becomes visible the typist can then begin a fresh sheet of paper and the pencil mark can be erased.

Another method is to draw a bold line across the backing sheet slightly above the point where the typing should finish. Unfortunately this method is not very effective when carbon copies are required, or when good quality paper is being used.

Enumerated items Sometimes paragraphs or items are numbered or lettered. The numbers or letters may stand on their own or be enclosed in brackets.

Spacing is as follows

eg 1 (2 or 3 spaces are left before typing)

A (2 or 3 spaces are left before typing)

(1) (2 spaces are left after the last bracket before typing)

Roman numerals can be used in enumerations. These may be blocked on the left or right

eg	Left	Right
	i	i
	ii	ii
	iii	iii

Decimal enumeration In addition to the other methods of enumeration it is quite common to use the decimal point followed by a figure for sub-division

eg 4.1
4.2
4.3
4.4

Leave two character spaces after the last figure before continuing typing.

Envelopes Begin typing a third of the way across the envelope and approximately half-way down. The name and address is usually typed in blocked style, although some firms prefer the indented style. When using the indented style it is important to indent each line the same number of spaces

eg James Brown Esq
4 High Street
SHEFFIELD
Yorkshire
S12 5PY

Special instructions such as URGENT, CONFIDENTIAL, PRIVATE, FOR THE ATTENTION OF, should be typed two single line spaces above the name of the addressee.

Only type the address in double spacing if the envelope is very large.

Each line of the address must occupy a separate line with the post town typed in CAPITALS.

The postcode, typed in BLOCKED CAPITALS, is always the last line of the address and should have a line to itself. One clear character space is left between the two halves of the postcode and no full stops or punctuation are required

eg Mr J Pearce
14 Linden Avenue
HARTHILL - Post town in CAPITALS
Derbyshire
SY1 2PT - Postcode in CAPITALS

See **Standard envelopes** for sizes of envelope and the size of paper they can accommodate.

Ergonomics The study of the relationship between workers and their environment.

Erratum In publishing, an item omitted from a book is acknowledged by the inclusion of an erratum slip.

Esquire (Esq) Use either Mr or Esq when addressing a man but never both.

In full punctuation the full stop is used to indicate an abbreviation eg `John Smith Esq` (open punctuation)

or `John Smith, Esq.` (full punctuation)

Exclamation mark This punctuation mark denotes an expression of some emotion. If not available on the typewriter, type an apostrophe, backspace one, then type a full stop

eg `!`

Fair copy The corrected typed copy of a rough draft, usually typed in double spacing.

Faulty shifting If a capital letter does not stand on the alignment scale a penalty is incurred in examinations. This error is known as faulty shifting.

Feed rollers These are small rubber rollers used to grip the paper in position.

Feet and inches It is permissable to use the apostrophe to represent feet and the double quotation marks to represent inches

eg `6' 4"`

A space is left between the feet and the inches.

Figures Use a comma or a space to mark millions and thousands in figures. Count in 3s from the right.

eg `1 000 000`
`1,000,000`

Commas are usually inserted in continuous text.

Fit The arrangement whereby the last line of each page of a typescript produced by several typists leads on without a break to the following sheet.

Flush paragraph Another name for a blocked paragraph, ie where every line begins at the same point.

Flush right – type that lines up vertically on the right

Flush left – type that lines up vertically on the left.

Followers The second and subsequent pages of a typescript.

Footnotes A note or comment at the foot of the page, referred to by a symbol in the text. The symbol used is sometimes raised in both the text and the footnote. Footnotes are typed so as to leave 1″ (25 mm) clear below. (Mark the paper before commencing to ensure the footnote falls in the correct position.)

If a ruled line is included before typing the footnote, this line is to extend from margin to margin with at least one clear line space above and below it.

In text leave no space before the figure or the sign. In the footnote at the bottom of the paper leave one character space after the figure or sign.

If there is more than one footnote leave one clear line space before typing the next footnote.

Footnotes are used

1 to give the source of a quotation used in a report

2 to give further explanation to the reader

3 to identify a reference or person mentioned in the body of the report.

Form letters Form letters are duplicated letters sent to customers with the appropriate details typed in.

These are generally used for routine matters which do not require an individual reply.

Fractions If the required fraction is not included on the keyboard then make up the easiest way

either	5/16	6/7
or	$\frac{5}{16}$	$\frac{6}{7}$

Both styles cannot be used together in the same task.

Where a whole number comes before a 'made up' fraction leave a space between the whole number and the fraction

eg 4 5/16

Fully blocked A style of typewriting where everything begins at the same point.

See also **Paragraphs**

Golfball printing element An interchangeable typing head which is shaped like a golf ball. As the keys are depressed the machine turns the head and the correct character strikes the ribbon. The golf-ball then moves along the paper as each key is depressed while the carriage remains stationary.

Grafting See **Stencils**

Guide keys Also referred to as 'home keys'. These are the eight keys which act as guides for the location of the rest of the keys in touch typing.

Half-space correcting This method of correction is used when it is necessary to substitute a word containing one more letter (or one less) than the word already typed.

Most machines have a special key for half-space correction but where this is not the case either the space bar or the back spacer can be used.

For example, to replace the word 'has' with 'have' –

Space bar method

(i) The whole word is erased

(ii) The carriage is moved to the space before the word

(iii) The space bar is held down, the first letter typed, and the space bar then released

(iv) Each letter is dealt with in this way

Back spacer method

(i) The whole word is erased

(ii) The carriage is moved to where the *second* letter has been typed

(iii) The back spacer is held down, the first letter typed, and the back spacer released

(iv) A space is added and the back spacer held down while the second letter is typed

(v) Each letter is dealt with in this way.

Half title This is the page which comes before the title page of a book and usually contains only the name of the book.

Hanging paragraphs See **Paragraphs**

Hard copy Anything written, typed or printed on paper from a computer/word processor.

Headed paper A4 or A5 paper which carries the company name, address, etc. Most examination boards supply their own headed paper to candidates.

Where headed paper is not available leave the following number of single line spaces from the top of the paper to allow for the letterhead:

A4 – (2″/50 mm) = 12 single lines

A5 – (1½″/38 mm) = 9 single lines

Headings

MAIN HEADING
(Leave 1 clear line space = 2 single line spaces)
Turn up at least 7 single line spaces from the top of the paper before typing the main heading. To commence typing turn up 2 single line spaces after the heading for the sub-heading or for the first paragraph.

Sub-heading
(leave 1 clear line space)
When typing in blocked style the sub-heading is typed at the left-hand margin. To commence typing turn up 2 single line spaces.

Centred Heading

The above is a centred heading which is centred over the typing line. See CENTRING HEADINGS OVER THE TYPING LINE.

This is a shoulder heading

This is an example of a shoulder heading. It could be typed as above or in capitals and the paragraph begins at the margin or is indented. Shoulder headings have a clear line space above and a clear line space below.

A paragraph heading. The paragraph starts on the same line as the heading. It may be blocked or indented and starts 2 or 3 character spaces after the heading.

Paragraph headings may run on without extra spaces after the last word, as in this example. If the heading is typed in lower case then it should be underscored.

SIDE OR MARGINAL HEADINGS	This is an example of a side or marginal heading. The paragraph may be blocked, indented or hanging. (See PARAGRAPHS). Remember to tap out the longest line in the marginal headings plus 2 or 3 spaces and set the tabulator stop.

Headings enclosed by the underscore – rules for typing

1 Type the first line and turn up *two* single line spaces

2 Type the heading

3 Turn up *one* single line space and complete the second line

eg ______________

TYPEWRITING

____

Only one single line space is left after the heading before typing the final line, because the underscore takes up very little space.

Start and finish the underscore under the first and last letters of the heading.

Hook-in This is a term used in connection with typing poetry. When there are too many words to go on a line, those at the end are placed above or below it to finish at the same point.

Horizontal characters across the paper

		Elite	*Pica*
A4 (297 mm × 210 mm)	approximately	140	115
A4 (210 mm × 297 mm)	approximately	100	82
A5 (landscape)	approximately	100	82
A5 (portrait)	approximately	70	60

Hot zone This is the area at the end of each line, a definite number of characters from the right-hand margin. The zone can be set by the typist, and words within this zone require hyphenation or they will be wrapped round, if the typewriter has that facility.

See also **Wraparound.**

House style This refers to a consistent style in which a particular firm has its letters, memos, etc typewritten.

Hyphen The hyphen has no space either side while the dash has one space either side.

Use the hyphen if two words can be joined together to form one word.

eg part-time

half-term

common-sense

The hyphen can also be used to represent 'to' as in

Sheffield-London
12-14 days

Identification Every typewriter has an identifying serial number which is given by the manufacturer.

Imperial paper sizes These are no longer commonly used but because most computers use a typeface which prints pica size there is a continuing demand.

Memo	8″ × 5″	205 mm × 127 mm
Octavo	5″ × 8″	127 mm × 205 mm
Sixmo	8″ × 6½″	205 mm × 165 mm
Quarto	8″ × 10″	205 mm × 254 mm
Foolscap	8″ × 13″	205 mm × 330 mm
Draft	10″ × 16″	254 mm × 410 mm
Brief	13″ × 16″	330 mm × 410 mm

Imperial weights Pounds and ounces are abbreviated to lb and oz. No 's' is added for the plural and one character space is left between figures and abbreviations.

eg 10 lb 9 oz

Inches See **Feet and inches**

Indented paragraphs See **Paragraphs**

Inserting the paper Some electronic typewriters are fitted with an automatic paper injector but on other models the paper has to be turned up by hand until it is in the right position for typing.

If paper is inserted crookedly, the paper release lever must be pulled forward. This removes the pressure of the feed rollers, which hold the paper against the platen, and enables the typist to adjust the paper freely.

Many typists move forward the paper release lever before taking paper out of the machine. This is a good habit, saves unnecessary wear on the platen and the feed rollers, and enables paper to be taken out of the typewriter less noisily.

Inset items These are items which are indented from the main text. Inset items may be used with any style of layout, the inset portion to be not less than 5 character spaces from the left-hand margin with a clear line space above and below.

When type is inset from the left-hand margin the longest line of the inset portion should end the same number of spaces from the right-hand margin.

When typing a business letter in an examination the student must remember to:

Inset [Read the instructions to see whether or not a carbon copy is required, and unless told otherwise insert the date.] Inset

Inside address This refers to the name and address of the addressee.

Instructions These might be handwritten, circled and/or prefixed 'typist'

eg (Typist)

Interliner This lever may be found on the right or left side of the platen. The interliner frees the platen from the rachet control so that the platen may be turned as required. When the lever is returned to its normal position the typewriter will automatically return to the original spacing.

The interliner is used for:

1 inferior and superior characters

2 double lines underneath totals

3 certain combination characters

4 typing on dotted lines

International paper sizes

A0	841 mm	×	1189 mm
A1	594 mm	×	841 mm
A2	420 mm	×	594 mm
A3	297 mm	×	420 mm
A4	210 mm	×	297 mm
A5	148 mm	×	210 mm
	210 mm	×	148 mm
A6	105 mm	×	148 mm
A7	74 mm	×	105 mm
A8	52 mm	×	74 mm
A9	37 mm	×	52 mm
A10	26 mm	×	37 mm

Inverted commas See **Double quotation marks**

Invoice This is a detailed list of goods delivered. An invoice is usually typed with many copies and NCR paper is often used to save time and trouble.

Items on an invoice are typed in single line spacing, with double between the items.

E & O E – this abbreviation means 'errors and omissions excepted'. Business documents often have these letters printed at the bottom and indicate that if a typist makes a mistake when typing the price on an invoice, this does not bind the seller.

Italic A special typeface whose characters have a noticeable inclination to the right. To indicate that a word should be typed in italics it is underscored.

Itinerary A typed schedule of an employer's appointments. If typed on a convenient sized piece of card it can be carried around easily.

eg I T I N E R A R Y

Schedule for 9 June 1986

10.00 am	Accounts Meeting Accountant's Office
11.30 am	J J Brownlow Co Ltd, West Street Manager - Mr James Black
2.15 pm	Social Club AGM Canteen
4.00 pm	R J White Ltd, Lilac Avenue Manager - Mr Peter Green

(The 24-hour clock could also be used.)

Junior and senior If 'Jun' (Junior) or 'Sen' (Senior) is used it is typed immediately after the name and before Esq

eg James Black Sen Esq (open punctuation)

or James Black, Sen., Esq. (full punctuation)

Justified right-hand margin To justify the right-hand margin (so that all the lines finish at the same point on the scale), a draft is required to assess the extra spaces needed between words to ensure that all lines end at the same point as the longest line.

To simply justify specific information at the right-hand margin, eg a date or an address, move the carriage to the right-hand margin and backspace one for each character and space.

Justifying The spacing out of every line to a predetermined width to obtain an even right-hand margin.

Keyboard, layout of

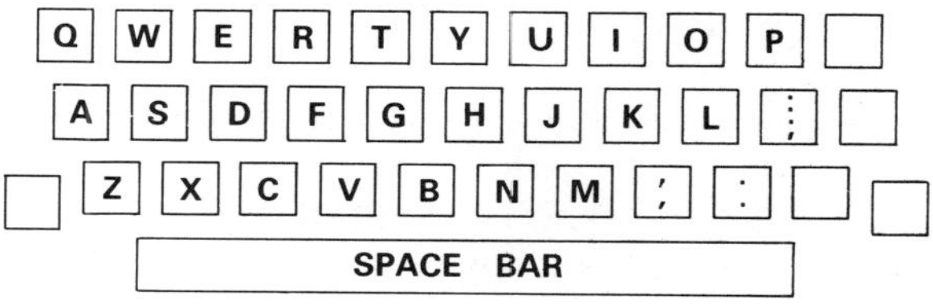

Keyboard layout

Keyboarding This is the act of inputting information by operating a keyboard. It is generally distinguished from 'typing' in that keyboarding does not have to result in hard copy whereas typing normally does.

Keypad A block of keys on a word processor or computer which, quite often, have dual functions.

Keystroke The act of depressing a key on a typewriter keyboard.

Landscape paper A5 paper (210 mm × 148 mm) inserted with the longer edge at the top.

Leader dots Leader dots are a series of dots usually used in tabulation to guide the eye from one column to another. They can be continuous or regularly placed single dots.

They must be aligned under each other with no more than four spaces between single dots or between groups of dots.

There must always be one space between the last word and the first dot and the last dot and further text.

One of the best rules to adopt is to make the dots and spaces add up to 5

eg 1 dot and 4 spaces
2 dots and 3 spaces
3 dots and 2 spaces

Left-hand margin Align the left-hand margin with the printed heading or leave a minimum of 1″ (25 mm) on A4 paper and ½″ (13 mm) on A5 portrait paper.

Legal Work A legal document is usually typed three times –

First typing – rough copy known as 'Draft'
Second typing – a neatly typed copy of the 'Draft' known as 'Fair Copy'

Third typing – the final copy, known as the 'Engrossment'

Most legal firms have their own house styles and many now use word processors.

General points to remember when typing legal documents:

1 a black ribbon is generally used

2 wide left-hand margin is required

3 most punctuation marks are omitted to avoid ambiguity

4 pages are numbered at the bottom

5 while the draft copy may be in treble spacing, generally the fair copy and the engrossment are typed in double spacing

6 no abbreviations are allowed and erasures are undesirable

Letters *Our ref* – contains the initials of the person who dictated the letter and those of the typist. The two parts are separated by a solidus. When 'Our Ref' is already printed on the letterhead, leave two character spaces before typing the initials and ensure that the alignment is correct.

Your ref – this is the reference on the letter being replied to. Leave blank if no reference given.

Date – every letter and memo has a date unless instructions state otherwise. Do not type the word 'Date', just the actual date. The date is usually typed day, month, year (eg 1 January 1988). The date in the text must be consistent with the date at the top of the letter.

Date as postmark – type this formula in place of the date.

URGENT, CONFIDENTIAL, PRIVATE – must be typed in capitals. See example on page 55.

Name and address of addressee – who the letter is to and his/her address.

Forms of address – decorations, honours and qualifications should always be in their correct order. As a general rule they are listed in order of importance

1 Decorations and honours

eg VC - Victoria Cross

2 Educational qualifications

eg MA - Master of Arts

3 Professional titles

eg FRSA - Fellow of the Royal Society of Arts

4 Member of Parliament – MP

Where an abbreviation consists of 2 or more letters with a full stop after each letter in full punctuation

eg F.R.S.A.

in open punctuation the full stops are omitted and no space is left between the letters

eg FRSA

However, one space (or comma) is required after each group of letters

eg VC MA FRSA

Post town – the post town is always typed in capitals and it never ends in 'shire'

eg CHESTERFIELD
Derbyshire

SHEFFIELD
Yorkshire

The post town is always typed at the beginning of a line unless the address appears in continuous text.

Postcode – leave a minimum of 2 and a maximum of 6 character spaces before the postcode when it appears on the same line as the last item of the address. One or two spaces are left between the two parts.

Attention line – the attention line is typed in closed capitals with or without underscore, or in lower case with underscore. It is typed after the date, leaving a minimum of one clear line space before and after it. If applicable ensure that the attention line is typed on the envelope. See **Attention line.**

Salutation – Dear ... (Sir, Madam, Mrs Brown, Nicola, etc).

Subject heading – sometimes placed in letters, showing what the body of the letter will be referring to.

Complimentary close – signing off the letter. Either 'Yours faithfully' or 'Yours sincerely'. However, when writing a letter to 'Dear Sir (or Madam)' always sign off 'Yours faithfully'.

Name of the firm – sometimes the name of the firm is typed directly under the complimentary close. This is usually typed in capital letters.

Name of signatory – typed name of the person who will sign the letter.

Designation – this states the company position of the person signing the letter (eg Sales Manager).

Enclosure – 'Enc' typed on the letter shows that one enclosure should be sent with the letter. Use 'Encs' if more than one enclosure is to be sent.

Open punctuation – a business letter typed in this style will have no punctuation in the reference, date, name and address of the addressee or salutation.

Punctuation is inserted as normal in the body of the letter but there is no punctuation in the complimentary close and any wording which follows the complimentary close. See **Paragraphs**; **Personal letters** and layout examples on the following pages.

Layout of a fully blocked letter

Reference -	Ref JB/PIB
	(Leave minimum of 1 clear line space)
Date -	4 October 1986
	(Leave minimum of 1 clear line space)
Addressee and Address -	Mr P Jones Marshall Tools Ltd 6 Commercial Street MANCHESTER M21 5RS
	(Leave minimum of 1 clear line space)
Salutation -	Dear Mr Jones
	(Leave minimum of 1 clear line space)
Subject Heading -	SALES FIGURES
	(Leave minimum of 1 clear line space)
	The final sales figures for the first three months of this year have now been calculated, and show a marked improvement on the corresponding period last year.
	Could you please circulate the enclosed information and ask all your Sales Personnel to come to Head Office next week, when we can discuss the figures in more detail.
	(Leave minimum of 1 clear line space)
Complimentary Close -	Yours sincerely
Name of Organisation -	PHILLIP MATHER LTD
	(Leave minimum of 4 clear line spaces)
Name of Signatory -	JIM BLACK
Designation -	Sales Director
	(Leave minimum of 1 clear line space)
Enclosure -	Enc

If a ‘CONFIDENTIAL’ line and/or ‘ATTENTION’ line has to be inserted, both the examples given are correct.

Ref MB/PIB
(Leave minimum of 1 clear line space)
22 March 1986
(Leave minimum of 1 clear line space)
CONFIDENTIAL
(Leave minimum of 1 clear line space)
Eagle Precision Ltd
18 Green Lane
LINCOLN
L19 6TY
(Leave minimum of 1 clear line space)
For the attention of Mr Peter Wood, Personnel Manager
(Leave minimum of 1 clear line space)
Dear Sir

Ref MB/PIB
(Leave minimum of 1 clear line space)
CONFIDENTIAL
(Leave minimum of 1 clear line space)
22 March 1986
(Leave minimum of 1 clear line space)
For the attention of Mr Peter Wood, Personnel Manager
(Leave minimum of 1 clear line space)
Eagle Precision Ltd
18 Green Lane
LINCOLN
L19 6TY
(Leave minimum of 1 clear line space)
Dear Sir

Fully blocked letter with open punctuation

Ref TW/PIB
(1 clear line space)
21 June 1986
(1 clear line space)
Mr James White
6 The Headrow
MANCHESTER
M18 5TR
(1 clear line space)
Dear Sir
(1 clear line space)

No punctuation required

Thank you for your letter of enquiry dated 16 June 1986.
(1 clear line space)
We have pleasure in enclosing the detailed information you require and if we can be of any further assistance do not hesitate to contact us.
(1 clear line space)
Yours faithfully
PHILIP MATHER LTD

(4 clear line spaces)

Thomas Mather
Managing Director
(Minimum of 1 clear line space)
Enc

No punctuation required

Fully blocked letter with full punctuation

Ref. TW/PIB

21st June, 1986

Mr. James White,
6 The Headrow,
MANCHESTER.
M18 5PY

Dear Sir,

Full punctuation required

Thank you for your letter of enquiry dated 16th June, 1986.

We have pleasure in enclosing the detailed information you require and if we can be of any further assistance do not hesitate to contact us.

Yours faithfully,
PHILIP MATHER LTD.

Thomas Mather
Managing Director

Enc.

Full punctuation required

Line spacing, examples of

This is an example of
text typed in single
line spacing.

This is an example of

text typed in one-and-a-

half line spacing.

This is an example of

text typed in double

line spacing.

This is an example of

text typed in treble

line spacing.

Lists/forms The word 'delete' means cross out. On the typewriter you can cross out by means of

a small 'x' for small letters
a capital 'X' for capital letters

eg ~~Cheque~~/postal order

Typing on dotted lines It is important to ensure that the 'tails' of letters (jgyq etc) just clear the line of dots

eg Peggy Smythe ....

Typing on continuous lines The same rules apply as for typing on dotted lines

eg Gerry Bright ____________________

When typing sums of money, figures, etc make sure the columns of tens, etc are correctly aligned units, if columns are to be totalled.

Totals Perhaps the easiest method is to underline the last item in the column, leave 1 clear line space and type the total, turn up 1 single line space and underscore. Turn up the machine very slightly (use interliner) and double score.

eg

6.75
1.25
1.50 Underscore last item
Leave 1 clear line space
£9.50 Type in total
Turn up 1 single line space ══ Underscore and use interliner for double lines

The following is also acceptable

eg

6.75
1.25
1.50 Underscore last item
Turn up 1½ line spaces ←
£9.50 Type in total
Turn up ½ line space ← ══ Underscore and use interliner for double lines

When typing the name and address along a single line using fully blocked layout and open punctuation, omit the comma and leave 2 character spaces between the items

eg

Mr James Black 4 High Street SHEFFIELD Yorkshire S12 5PY

When a dash is used in a column to represent 'nil' or 'not applicable' it must be consistently blocked, centred or typed under the units position, irrespective of style. One, 2 or 3 dashes are acceptable.

If boxes are provided, place the information in the centre of the box as far as possible.

Lists, typing of It is not necessary to centre lists vertically; all that is required is to leave a minimum of 6 clear line spaces between the top of A4 paper and the heading.

The longest line should be centred horizontally, and the left-hand margin set. All the lines then begin at the margin.

Literary work Good quality paper should always be used for literary work. Depending on the type of work, single, double or treble line spacing can be employed. No page number is required on the chapter page but second and subsequent pages are numbered as follows:

```
                     Turn up 4 single line spaces
                     (or 3 clear line spaces)

1" (25 mm)
in total                       2   (Type number)

                     Turn up 3 single line spaces
                     (or 2 clear line spaces)
                     to commence typing
```

Main headings This provides the subject heading for the letter. Leave at least 6 clear line spaces before typing the main heading, if not on headed paper, and at least one clear line space after the main heading for the sub-heading or text.

Maintenance Remove dust daily with a long handled brush.

Periodically brush the typeface with a stiff brush dipped in methylated spirits to remove surplus ink which eventually cloggs letters.

Always replace the typewriter cover at the end of the day, or when the typewriter is not in use.

If a fault develops always send for the mechanic – do not try to rectify it yourself.

Manifolding This term is applied to the making of several copies of the same material with carbon paper.

Margin release This is a key which temporarily releases both margins to allow work to be typed there.

Margin stops These stops are used to fix the points at which the lines of typing begin and end on the page.

Marginal headings see **Headings.**

Margins Important – the right-hand margin can be equal to the left-hand margin but never wider.

Top margin – a minimum of 1″ (25 mm) unless task centred vertically.

Left-hand margin – a minimum of 1″(25 mm) on A4 or A5 (landscape)
a minimum of ½″ (13 mm) on A5 (portrait)

Margins on a card – a minimum of ½″ (13 mm) all round.

Measurement of typing speed Typing speed is measured in words per minute (wpm). A 'word' for this purpose consists of 5 strokes or depressions of the keys. Each depression, character key or space bar, etc counts as one stroke.

eg A typing line of 60 spaces =
12 words (60 ÷ 5)

Speed is then calculated by dividing the number of words typed by the number of minutes taken, as

eg 300 words typed in 10 minutes
(300 ÷ 10) = 30 wpm

Measurements

(i) The letter 'x' is used for the word 'by'

eg `10 cm x 12 cm`

(ii) Abbreviations do not take an 's' in the plural

eg `4 ft`
`2 lb (Except litres and tonnes)`

and when using open punctuation there is no full stop after any abbreviation, except at the end of a sentence.

(iii) One space is left after the numbers before the unit of measurement

```
eg  10 (1 space) ft
     6 (1 space) in
```

(iv) A group of figures should never be separated at line endings.

Memorandum A memorandum or memo is a brief business note sent to a person, usually in the same firm. Wherever possible use a printed memorandum form.

Memos can be typed on A5 (landscape) or A4. Often you are asked to choose an appropriate size. If given instructions on which size to use, circle the size when reading through the examination paper.

Do not forget to type the date in full

eg `1 January 1987`

Margins should be aligned with the printed matter.

Example of memorandum

```
From:  (leave 2 spaces         Ref:   (leave 2 spaces
To:    after the longest       Date:  after the longest
       item before typing             item before typing
       insertion)                     insertion)
```

Leave one clear line space before typing heading or commencement of memo

Body of memo – usually typed in single line spacing with double between the paragraphs

If an enclosure is mentioned in the body of the memo it should be indicated by typing Enc (or Encs) in the bottom left-hand corner.

Menu In word processing a menu is a list displayed on a visual display unit (VDU) providing a choice of functions or items which may be selected by number or letter

eg WHAT WOULD YOU LIKE TO DO NEXT?

1 Edit a document
2 Print a document
3 Delete a document
4 Exit a program

PLEASE SELECT CHOICE BY NUMBER

Metric items When typing metric items leave one character space after the figure

eg 5 mm

Never add 's' to the symbol to form the plural

eg 1 mm - 6 mm

except when typing the plural of litre and tonne. These both have the 's' added to avoid confusion

eg 1 litre 6 litres
1 tonne 10 tonnes

Minus sign A hyphen with a character space before and after it is used to represent a minus sign

eg 4 - 2 = 2

However, if a minus quantity is to be shown the hyphen is placed close to the figure with one character space before it but no space after it

eg -8

Minutes These are recorded details of any decisions, resolutions or business discussed at a meeting which are kept for future reference.

Minutes are either written in a Minute Book or typed up for distribution.

Like the agenda, the heading for minutes includes the name of the organisation, type of meeting, place, date and time. A list of those present is recorded and each minute is numbered.

Minutes are typed single spacing with double between the items. Block or indented style and marginal headings are normally used.

Money, sums of

If only pounds are involved type £6 or £6.00
If only pence are involved type 6p, 81p
If mixed amounts are involved type £2.50 (do not use the abbreviation p for pence).

If the sum contains a decimal point but no whole pounds, a nought should be typed after the £ symbol and before the decimal point

eg £0.85p

Multiplication sign Use a small 'x' when typing the multiplication sign

eg 21 mm x 18 mm

Note that one character space is left before and after typing the multiplication sign.

Examples of minutes

I

(Leave minimum of 1 clear line space)

Minutes of a Committee Meeting of the Southdown Golf Club held in the Secretary's Office on 3 June 1986 at 1400 hours.

(Leave minimum of 1 clear line space)

PRESENT:

(Leave minimum of 1 clear line space)

Mr J Brown (Chairman)
Mr S Plant
Ms T Lane
Mrs A Bennett
Mr C Eyre
Mrs E Allsop
Mr V Black (Secretary)

(Leave minimum of 1 clear line space)

1	Apologies	Apologies were received from Mr G Turner and Mr B Payne.
	(Leave minimum of 1 clear line space)	
2	Minutes	Minutes of the AGM held on 6 May 1986 were approved and signed by the Chairman as a true record.
3	Matters arising	There were no matters arising.
4	Correspondence	A letter had been received from James Black Co Ltd asking for permission to use the Clubhouse facilities. After lengthy discussion it was agreed that permission would be granted.
5	Annual Outing	Mr Plant reported that the coach had been booked and the Safari Park had confirmed the reservation.
6	Winter Programme	Mr Eyre asked for all suggestions for the 1987 Winter Programme to be handed to him before the next meeting.
7	Any other business	Mr Lane raised the question of the repair to the boundary fence. Mrs Allsop said this was in hand.
8	Date of next meeting	The date of the next meeting to be 8 July 1986.

II

Minutes of a Committee Meeting of the Southdown Golf Club held in the Secretary's Office on 3 June 1986 at 1400 hours.

PRESENT:

Mr J Brown (Chairman)
Mr S Plant
Ms T Lane
Mrs A Bennett
Mr C Eyre
Mrs E Allsop
Mr V Black (Secretary)

1	Apologies	Apologies were received from Mr G Turner and Mr B Payne.
2	Minutes	Minutes of the AGM held on 6 May 1986 were approved and signed by the Chairman as a true record.
3	Matters arising	There were no matters arising.
4	Correspondence	A letter had been received from James Black Co Ltd asking for permission to use the Clubhouse facilities. After lengthy discussion it was agreed that permission would be granted.
5	Annual Outing	Mr Plant reported that the coach had been booked and the Safari Park had confirmed the reservation.
6	Winter Programme	Mr Eyre asked for all suggestions for the 1987 Winter Programme to be handed to him before the next meeting.
7	Any other business	Mr Lane raised the question of the repair to the boundary fence. Mrs Allsop said this was in hand.
8	Date of next meeting	The date of the next meeting to be 8 July 1986.

NCR (No Carbon Required) This is special paper treated with crystals and chalk which gives an automatic carbon copy. Often used in the preparation of invoices.

Advantages	*Disadvantages*
Clean to handle	More expensive
Quicker for the typist	Difficult to make corrections
Requires less storage space	Easy to mark accidentally

Notice of meeting A notice of a meeting is sent to everyone entitled to attend and includes the following information

day
time
place
and sometimes the purpose of the meeting

Try and remember to allow as many days warning as possible of the meeting.

Numbered/lettered paragraphs Always leave 2 or 3 character spaces after numbered/lettered paragraphs before beginning to type

eg 1 Words with a capital letter

A Carriage return drill

See also **Brackets**; **Enumerated items**

Numerals, Roman

Arabic	Capital Roman Numerals	Small Roman Numerals
1	I	i
2	II	ii
3	III	iii
4	IV	iv
5	V	v

Arabic	Capital Roman Numerals	Small Roman Numerals
6	VI	vi
7	VII	vii
8	VIII	viii
9	IX	ix
10	X	x
20	XX	xx
30	XXX	xxx
40	XL	xl
50	L	l
60	LX	lx
70	LXX	lxx
80	LXXX	lxxx
90	XC	xc
100	C	c
500	D	d
1000	M	m

Numeric pad This is a block of numbers on the keyboard arranged like a calculator and sometimes used in addition to the numbers above the letters.

Numerical order Items are arranged in order of number

eg 1, 2, 3 etc

Oblique sign (solidus) The oblique sign is used

1 for typing fractions not provided on the keyboard

eg 5/7 7/8

2 for addresses instead of the word 'and'

eg 2/4 Laurel Crescent

3 for telephone numbers with more than one line

eg 6438/9

4 in place of the word 'or'

eg he/she Mr/Mrs/Miss

5 in a reference on a letter

eg ACC/tab

There is no space before or after the oblique sign.

Omission of words See **Ellipsis**

Open punctuation This means that the full stop is omitted after abbreviations and that letters are typed without commas or full stops in the date, address, salutation and complimentary close.

Full punctuation is when all commas and full stops are inserted.

See also **Letters**

Ordinal numbers These denote order or sequence

eg 1st, 2nd, 3rd, 4th

They may be typed in words or figures.

Overtyping This is the practice of typing corrections over errors and should be avoided.

Paper guide This allows you to align the left-hand edge of the paper as it is inserted in the machine.

Paper release lever The paper may be adjusted by pulling this lever.

Paper sizes See also **Imperial paper sizes; Type sizes**

Character spaces across the paper

$$\begin{aligned} 1'' \text{ (25 mm)} &= \text{pica } 10 \\ &= \text{elite } 12 \end{aligned}$$

Line spaces down the paper

$$1'' \text{ (25 mm)} = \left.\begin{matrix}\text{pica}\\ \text{elite}\end{matrix}\right\} = 6$$

Paper/type sizes A5 paper with the shorter edge at the top indicates portrait paper.

A5 paper with the long edge at the top indicates landscape paper.

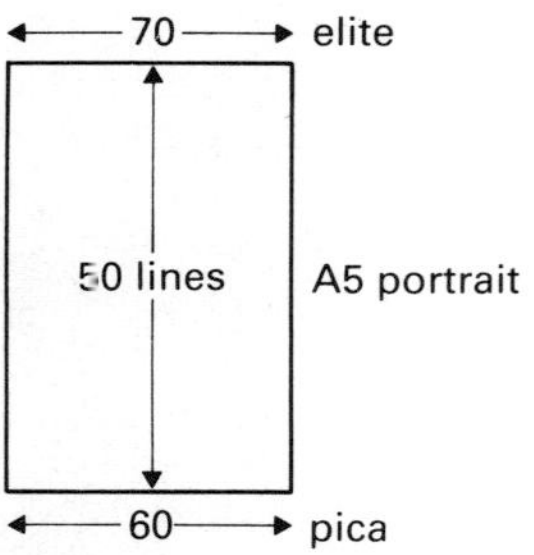

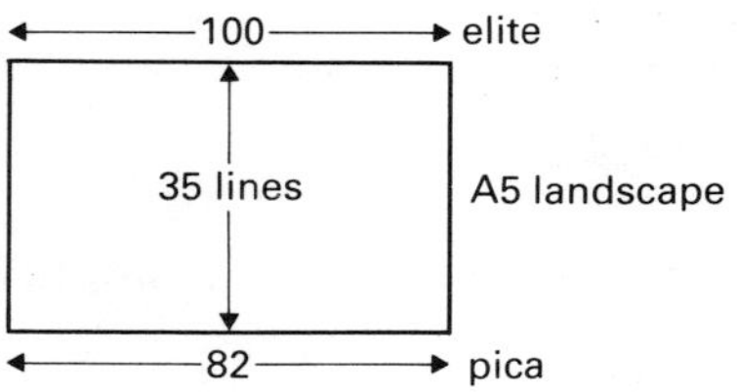

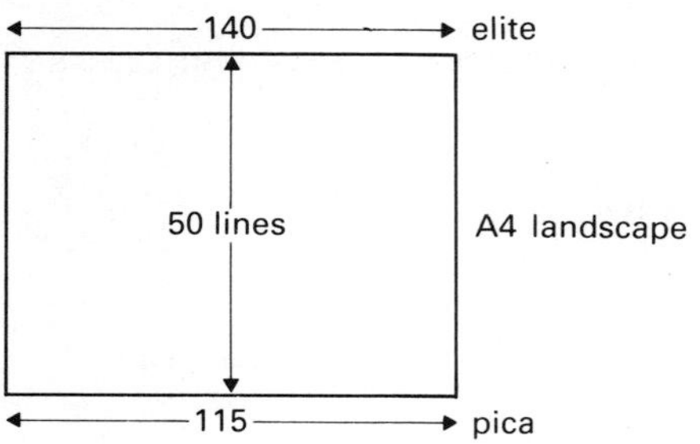

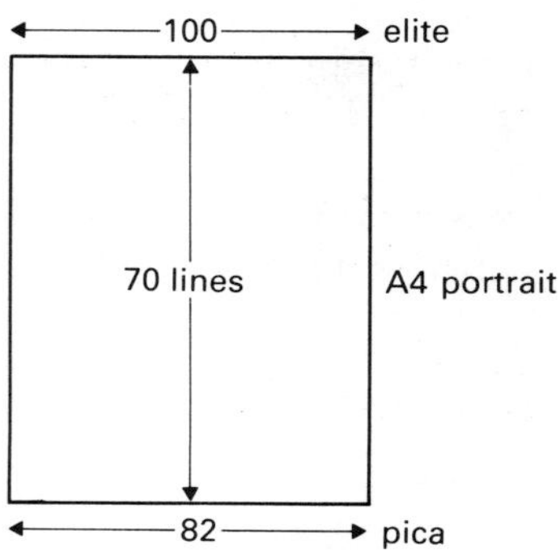

Paragraphs Turn up between paragraphs –

in single spacing – indented, blocked, hanging } 2 single spaces between each paragraph

in double spacing – indented – 1 double space

blocked – 2 double spaces

Different types of paragraphs

```
This is an example of a blocked paragraph; every
line starts at the margin.

     This is an example of an indented paragraph.
The first line of each paragraph starts five
character spaces in from the margin.

This is an example of a hanging paragraph.  The
  first line starts at the margin and subsequent
  lines begin two spaces in.
```

Parentheses See **Brackets**

Percentage sign No space is left between the figure and the percentage sign

eg 65%

Personal letters These can be typed on A4 or A5 paper, depending on the length of the letter.

Personal business letter A letter that is sent to a firm or an individual concerning a personal business matter. See example below.

Layout of personal letter

16 The Grove
BIRMINGHAM
B17 4LM
(Leave minimum of 1 clear line space)
20 August 1986
(Leave minimum of 1 clear line space)
Dear Michael
(Leave minimum of 1 clear line space)
I just heard your examination results and I thought I must write to congratulate you.

Knowing you, I expect you already have plans for your future and I would like to wish you every success in the area you choose to specialise in.
(Leave minimum of 1 clear line space)
Yours sincerely

Space for signature

Layout of personal business letter

12 Coniston Road ROCHDALE Lancashire R78 4WE	OR	12 Coniston Road ROCHDALE Lancashire R78 4WE
(Leave minimum of 1 clear line)		
3 June 1986	OR	3 June 1986

(Leave minimum of 1 clear line)

Green Lawns Garden Centre
Green Lane
BLACKPOOL
B12 6TY

(Leave minimum of 1 clear line)

Dear Sirs

(Leave minimum of 1 clear line)

I see from your advertisement in last week's edition of 'The Advertiser' that you have strawberry plants for sale.

Please send me 6 plants for which I enclose a cheque for £2.50.

Yours faithfully

(Leave minimum of 4 clear lines)

IAN MOORE

Usually a carbon copy is taken of a personal business letter.

Pica type There are 10 character spaces to 1″ (25 mm) in pica type.

Pitch This refers to the space occupied by a single character on the typewriter

eg elite = 12 to 1″ (25 mm)
pica = 10 to 1″ (25 mm)

Platen A rubber covered cylinder in the typewriter around which the paper is guided.

Plus sign If a plus quantity is to be shown the plus sign is placed close to the figure with a character space before the sign but no space after it,

eg +8

Poetry Type in single spacing with double or treble between the verses. Centre the longest line of the poem and commence all the lines at this point for blank verse and poems with all the lines rhyming. For poems with alternative lines rhyming, indent two or three character spaces for second, fourth, sixth lines.

The title is centred over the poem (See **Centring over the typing line**) and 2 clear line spaces are left before typing the first line.

The poet's name usually finishes at the same point as the longest line.

Portrait paper A5 (148 mm × 210 mm) paper inserted with the shorter edge at the top.

Postcards Postcards are sometimes used when the message is short and not private in content. The name and address of the firm is usually printed across the top of the postcard, and margins of ½″ (13 mm) are used.

When using blank postcards the firm's name and address are centred, beginning approximately ½″ (13 mm) from the top of the card.

After typing the address turn up 2 single line spaces to type the reference at the left-hand margin. The date is typed on the same line, flush with the right-hand margin.

Before typing the body of the postcard turn up 2 single line spaces.

Post town The destination town of a letter should always be typed in capitals.

See also **Letters.**

Poste restante This means 'to be called for' and is typed after the name of the addressee who will collect from the Post Office named in the address. Used for inland and overseas mail.

Postscript A postscript is an afterthought. It is usually abbreviated to PS and used only at the foot of a letter. It must have at least one clear line space above and can be typed before or after the word 'Enclosure'. A postscript is typed like a footnote, with a clear character space after the abbreviation.

Posture Good posture at the typewriter is essential. You should sit at right angles to the desk with feet on the floor, one foot slightly in front of the other. Wrists should neither be dropped nor arched but kept low, just clearing the typewriter.

Pound sign (£) The pound sign can be placed over the first figure in a pound column, or centred over the figure typing line.

eg	£	£
	126	126
	24	24
	145	145

Print carrier On an electronic typewriter this usually consists of the cassette ribbon, print head (daisywheel, golfball, etc), correction type and hammer unit, and travels along the platen.

Print head A printer will not work without a print head of some sort, usually a daisywheel or golfball, etc.

Printer's footnote Footnotes in typescript prepared for the printer should be inserted on the line following that in which the footnote appears.

To type a printer's footnote:

1. Turn up one single line space after the line in which the reference occurs.

2. Use the underscore to draw a line across the page.

3. Leave one clear line space and type the reference mark and footnote (one space is left after the reference mark before typing the footnote).

4. Turn up one single line space and draw a line.

5. Leave 1 clear line space to continue typing.

NB In the text there is no space before the figure or the sign.

Several footnotes which appear close to each other may be put together.

Printing point This is where the print head comes up to strike and print on the paper.

Proof reading This is checking typescript for errors.

Proportional spacing A feature whereby characters are allocated horizontal spacing in proportion to their size

eg 'l' occupies less space than 'w'

Punctuation The following are acceptable schemes for spacing after punctuation

Comma	1	1	1	1	1	1
Semi-colon	1	1	2	2	2	2
Colon	1	1	2	2	2	2

Full stop/ question mark/ exclamation mark at the end of a sentence	1 2 3 2 2 3

Question mark Leave 1, 2 or 3 spaces after a question mark but no space between the preceding word and the question mark

eg `How are you feeling?`
`Shall we go home?  Yes, please.`

Quire This is one-twentieth of a ream and contains 24 sheets of paper.

See also **Ream**

Quotation marks (double) Leave no space between speech and the quotation marks used before and after it

eg `"This is mine", said James.`

Qwerty The standard layout of a keyboard device, so called because the first six characters on the second line are Q W E R T Y.

Ream A ream consists of 480 sheets of paper. Most typewriting paper is sold in reams.

Receipts and payments account This may be used by a club or society to show, in summarized form, the amounts of cash paid out during a given period and the amount of cash in hand. Type as you would a single-sheet balance sheet.

See also **Balance sheet**

Reference The reference consists of, first, the initials of the person who dictated the letter, second, those of the typist. The two parts are separated by a solidus

eg `PIB/MB`

Reference numbers Reference numbers on documents are sometimes quoted in letters for quick access to the relevant correspondence

eg `Employee No 67687`

Relocate A special key found on an electronic typewriter. When this key is depressed the carriage returns to the previous position.

Rep An abbreviation of the word 'representative'.

Repeat key (automatic) A function available on some typewriters which allows a character to be repeated continuously.

Reprography This means any method of reproducing a document, eg photocopying.

Ribbon indicator Colour coded for easy recognition

eg black (or blue)
white
red

When set at black the top half of the ribbon is used for typing and when set at red the bottom half is used. The white position disengages the ribbon for stencil work, etc.

See also **Stencils**; **Disengaging the ribbon**

Ribbons *Fabric Ribbon* – made of inked fabric. Can be used until the ink fades but it does not produce a very clear image.

Carbon ribbon – ribbon backed with a carbon film. Produces a much sharper impression than that usually achieved with a fabric ribbon, but can only be used once.

Monochrome ribbon – only one colour.

Bi-chrome ribbon – combination of two colours, usually black and red, although other colours are available.

Right-hand margin The right-hand margin should be kept as even as possible. The overall impression should not be that the right-hand margin is wider than the left.

See also **Justified right-hand margin**

Roller (for paper) See **Platen**

Roman numerals All Roman numerals are formed from the following seven symbols

eg `I(1)` `X(10)` `C(100)` `M(1,000)`

`V(5)` `L(50)` `D(500)`

Any unit symbol can be repeated two or three times

eg `II` `III`

A letter placed *before* one of greater value indicates that the first is subtracted from the second to find the sum

eg `XC = 90`
`10 - 100 = 90`

A letter placed *after* one of greater value indicates that both are added to find the sum

eg `CX = 110`
`100 + 10 = 110`

Small Roman numerals are produced using small letters

eg `i, ii, iii, iv`

Large Roman numerals are produced using capital letters

eg `I, II, III, IV`

This is a capital 'i', not the 'l' key.

Follow the typing size instructions given in the draft.

Roman numerals can be blocked from left to right

eg i
ii
iii
iv

or from the right to the left

eg I
II
III
IV

Uses of Roman numerals – Large Roman numerals are used for

1 expressing the year

eg MCMXXXVI

2 names of Monarchs

eg Henry VIII

3 class or form numbers

eg Class IV V Form

4 books of the Bible

eg II Samuel

5 numbering headings, sections and chapters in a play

eg CHAPTER III

6 clock faces

7 enumerating paragraphs

eg `Paragraph IV`

Small Roman numerals are used for –

1 paginating prefaces

eg `page i of the preface`

2 sub-paragraphs, sub-sections and appendices

eg `appendix viii`

3 chapters in the Bible

eg `I John iii, 20`

Ruled table In a ruled table the column headings are separated from the column items by horizontal lines. Vertical lines can also be used.

See also **Headings**; **Boxed tables**

Salutation This refers to 'Dear Sirs' etc, ie the opening line of a business/personal letter.

Seconds (time) The word 'second' can be abbreviated by typing the double quotation sign after the figure

eg `20"`

Semi-blocked letter A semi-blocked letter differs in the following ways to a fully blocked letter –

1 The date is backspaced from the right-hand margin.

2 The heading is centred over the typing line. See **Centring over the typing line**

3 Paragraphs are indented (the first line of each paragraph begins 5 character spaces in from the margin). See **Paragraphs**

4 Complimentary close, etc all begin at the centre of the typing line.

Layout of semi-blocked letter

Ref JD/PLM 12 May 1986

(Leave minimum of 1 clear line)

James Kinder Co Ltd
Chesterfield Road
SHEFFIELD
Yorkshire
S12 4JP

Date back spaced from right-hand margin.

(Leave minimum of 1 clear line)

Dear Sirs

(Leave minimum of 1 clear line)

COMPUTER HARDWARE

Heading centred over typing line

(Leave minimum of 1 clear line)

Indented → Thank you for your letter of 9 May 1986. We shall be pleased to arrange for our Sales Manager, Mr James Dean to call at your office to give you a demonstration of our computer hardware.

(Leave minimum of 1 clear line)

Indented → If you will kindly let us know a date that would be convenient to you, we shall then be able to make the necessary arrangements.

(Leave minimum of 1 clear line)

Yours faithfully
COMPUTER SUPPLIES LTD

(Leave minimum of 4 clear lines)

J Dunn
Managing Director

Semi-blocked letter with full punctuation

Ref. JD/PLM 12th May, 1986

James Kinder Co. Ltd.,
Chesterfield Road,
SHEFFIELD,
Yorkshire.
S12 4JP

Dear Sirs,

COMPUTER HARDWARE

Thank you for your letter of 9th May, 1986. We shall be pleased to arrange for our Sales Manager, Mr. James Dean to call at your office to give you a demonstration of our computer hardware.

If you will kindly let us know a date that would be convenient to you, we shall then be able to make the necessary arrangements.

Yours faithfully,
COMPUTER SUPPLIES LTD.

J. Dunn
Managing Director

Senior See **Junior and senior**

Signatory This is the person who signs a letter. In many instances the name is typed underneath in case the signature cannot be read.

Solidus See **Oblique**

Spacing To leave 3 clear line spaces always turn up 4.

If you are asked to leave a clear 1″ (25mm), turn up 7 single spaces

eg 25 mm (1") = 6 + 1 line to type on = 7

Line space indicator On some machines you must make sure that the whole of the figure is in the line space indicator box, remembering that the line space indicator moves in half lines.

Special marks (urgent, confidential, private) These are typed at the top of a document that requires special attention. They are typed in capitals or underlined with a clear line space above and below. The same rules apply for typing special marks on envelopes and care must be taken to ensure that when a letter bears a special mark this is also included on the accompanying envelope.

Special signs/symbols See **Combination characters**

Specifications This document details the work which a contractor proposes to undertake on any particular job, itemising how the work is to be carried out and what materials are to be used.

Most firms have their own house styles and the following examples are to be used simply as a guide to the style used by engineers and builders.

Engineers' specification – Indented style

S P E C I F I C A T I O N
(Leave 1 clear line space)
of work required to be executed
(Leave 1 clear line space)
in the erection of steel fencing

Centred over paper

(Leave 3 clear line spaces)

4 October 1986

(Leave 2 clear line spaces)

P R E L I M I N A R I E S

(Leave 2 clear line spaces)

MATERIALS All materials to be exactly as specified as no substitute will be accepted.

Indented Paragraphs

Blocked style

All blocked at left-hand margin

S P E C I F I C A T I O N
(Leave 1 clear line space)
of work required to be executed
(Leave 1 clear line space)
in the erection of steel fencing

(Leave 3 clear line spaces)

4 October 1986

(Leave 2 clear line spaces)

P R E L I M I N A R I E S

(Leave 2 clear line spaces)

MATERIALS All materials to be exactly as specified as no substitute will be accepted.

Builders' specification – Indented style

S P E C I F I C A T I O N of work to
(Leave 1 clear line space)
be done in connection with the
(Leave 1 clear line space)
erection of a church at London Road.

(Leave 2 clear line spaces)

James Henson ARIBA
Architect
66 West Street
BLACKPOOL
Lancashire
B18 6YX

(Leave 3 clear line spaces)

5 January 1987

(Leave 2 clear line spaces)

P R E L I M I N A R I E S → Heading centred over typing line

(Leave 2 clear line spaces)

Indented Paragraphs

SITE The site is situated on the corner of London Road, Blackpool and can be inspected at any time.

Block style The main heading is blocked at the left-hand margin and the body of the Specification is typed in blocked style.

Square brackets To type a square bracket use the following guide –

Left bracket

1 Type the oblique sign, backspace one and type the underscore.

2 Turn the platen back one full line space and type the underscore.

3 Turn the platen up one single line space, backspace once and continue typing until you get to the right bracket.

Right bracket

1 Type the oblique sign, backspace 2 and type the underscore.

2 Turn the platen back one full line space and type the underscore.

3 Turn the platen up one single space. This will produce

Standard envelopes

Type of envelope	Size of envelope	A4 paper	A5 paper
C7/6	162 mm 81 mm 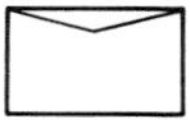		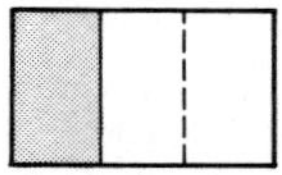 folded twice
C7	114 mm 81 mm 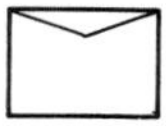	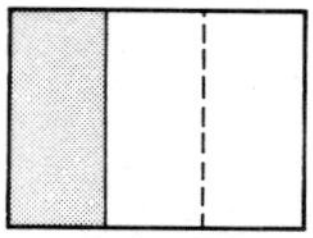 folded twice	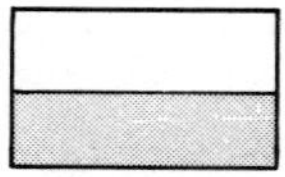 folded once
C6	162 mm 114 mm 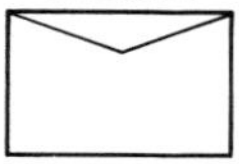	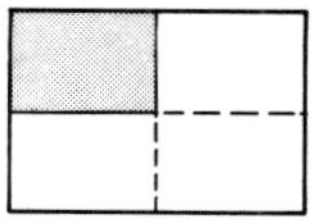 folded twice	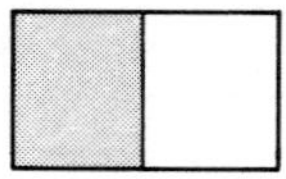 folded once
C5	229 mm 162 mm 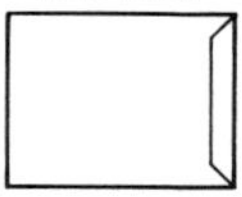	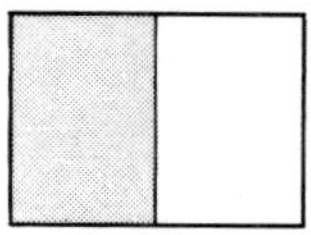 folded once	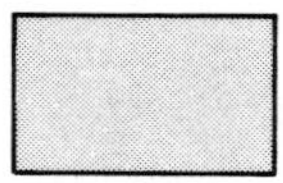 unfolded
C4	324 mm 229 mm 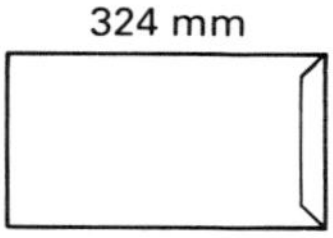	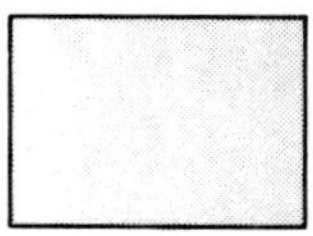 unfolded	

Standard sizes of paper

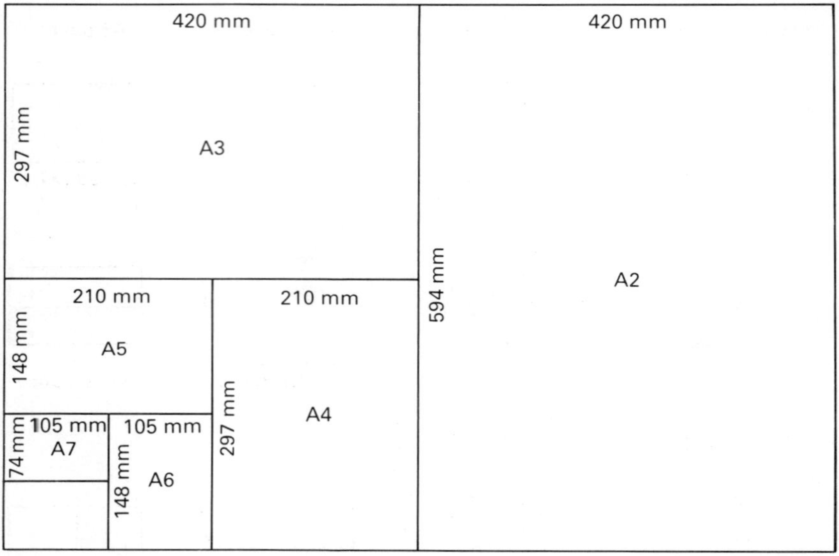

A2 420 mm × 594 mm
A3 420 mm × 297 mm
A4 210 mm × 297 mm
A5 (portrait) – 148 mm × 210 mm
A5 (landscape) – 210 mm × 148 mm
A6 148 mm × 105 mm

Statement This is a document sent to the customer at the end of each month showing how much has been paid to the supplier during the month, how much has been bought and any credit due.

Stencils A stencil is used to reproduce typescript. When preparing a stencil the ribbon should be disengaged (see **Disengaging ribbon**) to allow the keys to hit the stencil directly.

Corrections on stencils For small corrections use stencil correcting fluid. It is important to let it dry thoroughly before typing in the correct word(s). It is advisable to insert a pencil between the wax stencil and the backing sheet when making corrections to prevent the fluid sticking the stencil to the backing sheet. Care must be taken to ensure that additional pressure is used to cut through the extra thickness of wax. The keys must be cleaned after typing a stencil to remove the wax.

Grafting When considerable alteration is required the whole of the incorrect portion should be cut out with a sharp knife and the correct typing, previously typed on a spare piece of stencil, should then be substituted. To secure the graft, paint the edges with stencil varnish.

Stencils – electronic machines Before typing the ribbon is removed.

Stylus This is the name given to the 'pen' used for signatures and drawings on a stencil.

Stet See **Correction signs**

Sub-heading Turn up 1 clear line space after the main heading for the sub-heading. After typing the sub-heading turn up a minimum of 1 clear line space.

Superior/inferior characters Superior characters are typed half a line space above the line of type and inferior characters half a line space below.

eg Superior characters 50°

Inferior characters H_2O

Remember to return to the line of type when the special character has been typed.

Superscripts/subscripts See **Superior/inferior characters**

Tabulation *Simple rules for tabulation* –

1 Remove all margins and tabulator stops.

2 Insert the paper so that the edge of the paper is level with '0' on the paper bail.

3 Put the printing point at the edge of the paper.

4 Tap out (on the space bar) one for every character and space in the longest item in the first column.

5 Tap out the spaces required between the columns (usually 3 or 5).

6 Tap out the longest item in the second column and add the spaces between the column.

7 Continue tapping out the remaining columns in the tabulation. (Remember – no spaces are required after the last column.)

8 Check to see where the printing point has stopped with regard to the paper bail.

9 Deduct this number from the number of spaces across the paper and then divide by 2. The result gives you your left-hand margin.

10 Set the left-hand margin and continue, as before, from the commencement of the left-hand margin, to tap out the characters and spaces in the longest item in the first column. Add the spaces between the columns and press the tabulator stop key.

11 Continue across the paper, remembering to press the tabulator stop key after each column plus the spaces.

Two common faults

1 The paper has not been inserted at '0' on the paper bail.

2 Previous tabulator stops were not removed.

See also **Boxed table**; **Ruled table**

Tabulation in continuous matter This should be centred or blocked at the left-hand margin according to the style adopted in the continuous matter, and should be completed within one page.

Example of simple tabulation

Student's Name	Date of Birth	Course No
(Leave 2 clear line spaces		
Margaret Adams	22.3.70	6170
Andrew Butler	8.9.70	6172
Dean Carter	9.2.69	6181
Sarah Marks	12.3.69	6171
Jane Ford	1.6.70	6170

Double line spacing

Example of a tabulation in a memorandum

MEMORANDUM

(Leave 2 clear line spaces)

From: Chief Purchasing Officer   Ref: SH/BIS

(Leave 1 clear line space)

To: Financial Officer   Date: 8 May 1986

Sometimes no line space is left.

(Leave 2 clear line spaces)

Tabulated below are the further financial details you requested at our meeting yesterday.

(Leave 1 clear line space)

Current salary wage costs are as follows:

(Leave 1 clear line space)

Central Store	7 current posts	£65,655
Packing Stores and Despatch	8 current posts	£63,189
Divisional Stores	4 current posts	£19,904
Site Maintenance	9 current posts	£40,494

Example of tabulation with vertical headings

Turn up 2 single line spaces →

	Shorthand 50-70 wpm	Shorthand 70-100 wpm	Shorthand 100-140 wpm	Typewriting Elementary	Typewriting Intermediate	Typewriting Advanced
October	20	6	18	11	4	13
March	21	16	14	30	5	22
May	8	10	12	18	3	26
June	9	14	7	25	17	3

Turn up 1 single line space →

See also **Vertical headings**

Example of tabulation with diagonal headings

Turn up 2 single line spaces after line →

	English	Commerce	Accounts	Maths	Typing	Shorthand	Law
M Green	78	90	56	45	78	89	90
J Wainwright	64	87	54	56	65	87	85
P Fairbrother	54	62	51	45	87	64	92
J Black	53	64	73	81	36	74	53
M Snowdon	43	76	32	64	73	74	54
W Smith	63	67	56	74	51	45	63

Turn up 1 single line space before line →

Tabulator This is used to fix given point(s) on the typing line. The position of the tabulator varies with different machines.

Tail piece A decorative arrangement at the end of a typescript.

See also **Borders, ornamental**

Thimble A printing element shaped like a thimble.

Tilde (~) This sign placed over a letter 'n' in a Spanish word indicates it should be pronounced as if followed by 'y'.

Time Use figures with am and pm but words or figures can be used with o'clock. A full stop separates the hours from the minutes

eg	6.30 pm	1.20 am
	6 o'clock	six o'clock

The 24-hour clock begins at 0001 hours and ends at 2359 hours. Always use four digits and no full stop between the hours and the minutes. The four unpunctuated figures in the time should be followed by the word 'hours'.

Any time up to 1159 hours indicates the morning period, and the afternoon, evening and night periods begin at 1200 hours and continue until 2359 hours.

Midnight is referred to as 0000 hours.

Top margin On A4 paper leave a clear 1″ (25mm) before commencing typing, ie turn up 6 clear line spaces

Totals See **Lists/forms**

Travel itinerary This covers a given period of time, indicates where a person will be on any given day, and lists the activities for the day.

Treeing This term is used to indicate the tree-like marks on a carbon copy, caused by using a creased carbon.

Type bars These are the bars which lie in a curved shape in the 'well' of the manual typewriter. Each type bar has a face bearing characters which corresponds with the key tapped.

Type basket Nest of type hammers which is the print mechanism in a manual typewriter.

Type sizes

Character spaces across the paper

1″ (25 mm) = pica 10
= elite 12

Line spaces down the paper

1″ (25 mm) = pica } = 6
elite }

Typeface The design of a particular set of type. Numerous types are available and on some typewriters the typeface is interchangeable.

Typescript This is the term used for work produced on a typewriter.

Typewriter, care of

1 Cover the machine when not in use.

2 Always use a backing sheet to protect the platen.

3 Move the carriage to either left- or right-hand side when rubbing out to prevent dust falling into the machine.

4 Clean daily or at least once a week.

5 When carrying a typewriter

(i) keep the back of the machine nearest to you

(ii) make sure that the carriage is locked (place both margins at the centre of the carriage)

(iii) never lift the machine by the carriage.

Typewriters – *Manual machine* To use a manual typewriter the typist must strike the keys so that the typeface hits the ribbon and prints the character of the key struck.

Electric machine An electric typewriter gives a firm, even impression regardless of the pressure of the keys, thus making electric typewriters less tiring than manual. Automatic features such as repeat keys increase the typist's speed. Some electric typewriters have type bars similar to the manual machine but many have an interchangeable printing element which give a wide range of type styles without changing the machine.

Electronic machine Electronic typewriters usually have a memory facility and automatic correction. They enable the typist to work faster and are usually very reliable.

Typing pool This is where all (or most) of the typists in an organisation work in one room together instead of in separate offices, and where the work is shared among them.

Typist One whose prime responsibility is to operate a typewriter.

Typographical errors Typographical errors are characters that are wrongly typed and not corrected. Remember to check carefully before removing from the typewriter.

Underscoring headings Headings in *closed capitals* may or may not be underscored – follow the draft.

Headings in *spaced capitals* may or may not be underscored – follow the draft.

Headings in lower case with initial capital letter(s) MUST be underscored.

u/s or US means underscore.

Do not underscore punctuation at the end of a heading.

Headings underscored in draft Single line under heading indicates underscore as normal

eg Revision = Revision

Double line under heading indicates that the heading is to be typed in *blocked capitals* – do not double underscore the heading

eg Revision = REVISION

Treble line under heading indicates that the heading is to be typed in *spaced capitals*

eg Revision = R E V I S I O N

Unfamiliar/unclear words If a word is unfamiliar a dictionary might prove useful. If, however, a word is difficult to read, adopt the following procedure –

1 Look elsewhere in the document to see if you can find the same shape letters as in the word.

2 Read the whole paragraph and try to get the gist of the sentence.

3 Leave the task for a while, read through another piece and then return to the offending word.

Upper case See **Capitals**

Variable line spacer This is found on either the left or right platen knob. By pressing this button the platen can be moved to any position you require.

The variable line spacer is used for –

1 typing on dotted lines

2 double lines under a total

3 to obtain the original typing line when reinserting paper.

Vertical headings Vertical headings are used when columns are too narrow to type the headings horizontally. The columns should all be the same width as the longest item. When calculating the number of lines to leave for the vertical headings it is important to remember that 6 single lines down the paper is equal to 1″, this being equivalent to 12 character spaces in elite type (10 in pica).

Another method of finding the amount of space required for vertical headings is to type the longest heading on a piece of paper and measure the space needed.

Vertical line spacing Vertical line spacing is exactly the same for elite and pica type

eg	A4 (297 mm × 210 mm)	– 50 single line spaces down
	A4 (210 mm × 297 mm)	– 70 single line spaces down
	A5 (landscape)	– 35 single line spaces down
	A5 (portrait)	– 50 single line spaces down

Warning bell/bleep A bell or bleep is heard several spaces before the right-hand margin stop to warn you that you have only a few spaces left on which to type. The number of spaces varies on different typewriters.

If necessary you may use the margin release key to complete a short word.

See also **Margin release**; **Hot zone**

Weights See **Imperial weights**

Widow and orphan lines These terms refer to odd lines, such as the first line of a new paragraph appearing at the end of a page, or the last line of text appearing on its own on a continuation sheet. They are to be avoided.

Window envelopes Window envelopes save time in that the letter is folded in such a way that the inside name and address can be seen through the window. This also avoids the possibility of an error occurring when the address is typed on the envelope.

See also **Envelopes**; **Inside address**

Words in boxes Certain unclear words are sometimes written in the margin

eg SEPARATE

Type as shown in the text, not necessarily in capital letters.

Words or figures

General rules:

1 Type all numbers as figures except

(i) the number 'one'

(ii) a number at the start of a sentence

These two exceptions must always be typed as words.

or 2 Type one to nine in words and the remainder in figures.

Where it is essential to ensure accuracy or prevent fraud (ie cheques, legal documents) both words and figures are used

eg `We promise to pay, three hundred pounds (£300).`

Remember, whichever option you choose, be consistent.

Wraparound This is a facility which automatically transfers a word that is too long for the line of type on to the next line.

See also **Hot zone**